W9-BTD-609

The Absolute Beginner's Book of House Plants

The Absolute Beginner's Book of House Plants

by LEE LESTER

Foreword by JULIE MORRIS

Photographs by JOEL LEVINSON

The Citadel Press   Secaucus, N. J.

Library of Congress Cataloging in Publication Data

Lester, Lee.
  The absolute beginner's book of house plants.

  Includes index.
  1. House plants. I. Title.
SB419.L42   635.9'65   75-14312
ISBN 0-8065-0473-0

Copyright © 1975 by Lee Lester
All rights reserved
Published by Citadel Press
A division of Lyle Stuart, Inc.
120 Enterprise Ave., Secaucus, N. J. 07094
In Canada: George J. McLeod Limited
73 Bathurst St., Toronto, Ont.
Manufactured in the United States of America
Designed by William R. Meinhardt

To

My Creative Donald

Acknowledgments

During the days of The Potting Shed, Julie Morris was our horticultural consultant. We valued her knowledge and advice but it is to a special quality I wish to pay tribute: she has a love for plants so deep, encompassing and quietly committed, that it seems to give her kinship with them. It is a quality which, fortunately, I became aware of and was able to watch and enjoy.

Indebtedness to the people who came to The Potting Shed must also be acknowledged. Because there were hundreds, they must be nameless except for one like the boy, Alfred, thirteen years old and already so passionately involved with plants that all his baby-sitting funds were earmarked for The Potting Shed. From these people's need to care for and to cherish plants I developed an infinitely more tender relationship with our green world.

There are three people who can be named: Mrs. Ernesta Ballard, Executive Director of The Pennsylvania Horticultural Society, whose uncompromising standard of excellence was the source of inspiration and emulation in The Potting Shed and continues to be our standard for our private collection.

And Mrs. Sidney Keith, from whom I learned that an obstinate plant can be taught to relax pleasurably and beautifully in a hanging basket.

I wish also to express my appreciation to Mr. Peter A. Hyypio, Extension Botanist at Cornell University—U.S. Department of Agriculture, for his patient and detailed scrutiny of the list of plants I submitted to him for verification of nomenclature.

6

Contents

8   *Contents*

List of Illustrations

9

The Absolute Beginner's
Book of House Plants

Foreword

The art of gardening in containers is many thousands of years old. Whether practiced indoors or out this phase of horticulture has brought to many people the pleasure and peace of mind provided by life surrounded by green, growing things.

Since the first Earth Day in 1970 I have noticed a tremendous increase of interest in growing plants. Most of us live in urban areas where the space available for gardening is limited. House plants answer the need for many to grow something. Some people can put their indoor plants outside in the summer and add to their number with pots of vegetables and summer bedding plants. However, for many of us the house will be our only gardening area. Even if outdoor gardening space is available, house plants are a valuable part of our gardening experience as they provide year round enjoyment and brighten the winter months.

Nothing is more discouraging to the house-plant gardener than buying a plant in prime condition and then watching it deteriorate. Even allowing for the period of shock most plants go through when moved from greenhouse to house culture, we all know the signs that go beyond this temporary condition. No new growth appears, lower leaves yellow and fall off, and eventually the plant dies. Why?

Most of the questions I answer in my work with the Pennsylvania Horticultural Society concern house plants. Watering seems to cause more concern than any other part of the cultural requirements. Yet the indoor gardener needs to know and understand the proper balance of the three main requirements of house-plant culture; light, temperature and humidity.

Years of experience in The Potting Shed, the greenhouses which Lee Lester and her husband Donald conducted, have given her the insight to know that most of her customers really didn't know *why* they should water some plants more than others or *why* they should cut their plants back or *why* they should fertilize their plants to keep them in good condition. Most beginning gardeners need to go beyond the "how to" of things and understand the "why."

The Absolute Beginner's Book of House Plants is a house-plant primer for the beginner who grows plants in pots. Understanding this book doesn't mean you will never again have a house-plant failure. We all experience plants dying for seemingly unaccountable reasons. However, this primer introduces you to the basic needs of house plants and *why* they are necessary. How to select plants for your own situation, what plants to choose, and the cultural requirements for their continued flourishing growth are a few of the subjects covered.

Growing a plant in a pot means that the gardener has assumed the responsibility for that plant and that she must continue to care for that plant to keep it healthy and beautiful. Fourteen years of experience with gardening in containers has made this form of gardening my favorite. The enjoyment is boundless and the possibilities of all the combinations of plant form, leaf shape, color and texture provide endless interest and variety.

Lee Lester teaches the readers of this book the practical

knowledge needed by beginners to grow house plants successfully and leaves them with the subtle implications and
understanding of this phase of plant culture as part of the
broader art of gardening.

Julie Morris
March 1975

BEGONIA, scharffii

Introduction

For many years we operated commercial greenhouses called The Potting Shed. They were unique in the Delaware Valley for the variety of unusual plants available to the public. Our publicity proclaimed the fact that in an age of anxiety with wars and rumors of wars, plants in the home are an important link to the eternal realities and verities of Nature and that today there is a wide range of unusual and exotic varieties that are proved house-hardy and that are easy to care for and a pleasure to live with.

Certainly then, plants should not be a source of additional anxiety even for the beginner. From the very start of the beginner's horticulture career, plants should be an experience of joy and wonder at growth, at the beauty of leaves unfolding and flowers freshly coming into bloom. Plants should enrich the life of the beginner. Plants should add to the excitement of planning the decoration of a home, of devising ingenious ways to make a drab and dark corner a magnet for every eye with a magnificent specimen plant living very comfortably in that corner with two spotlights shining down upon it. Plants mean valuable lessons for young children which they get in no other way and finally, plants should add to the serenity of life.

19

And yet, we remember the feeling of unease when we started our adventure in horticulture. We purchased eight three-inch pots of philodendron, the vine with the heart-shaped leaf which you can buy in the five-and-ten or in the supermarket. We put them in our Dutch sink in the dining room and kept them alive without knowing exactly how we did it. Each year, however, they looked less and less attractive—their leaves grew smaller and their vines grow limp and straggly. After a few years, they were no longer an asset to the room and we discarded them.

We missed them. We realized that they had added not only to the appearance of the Dutch sink, but had contributed a different dimension to our home—a green vibrancy quite distinct from the charm of beautiful furniture and books. The plants had contributed the element of growth and change. We wanted more plants—philodendron and other varieties— but we did not want to buy plants only to witness their gradual demise. Now we wanted knowledge. By this time we had learned that plants should be fed (we had starved our philodendron). We had heard someone talk about pinching out and pruning, but we did not know what that meant. We did not know why bathing a plant was essential. If we had been told then that a plant breathed, we really would have been amused. We had at one time seen plant polish advertised in the store and we had bought it and applied it liberally to both sides of the leaves. We did not know that was forbidden. We had noticed a white substance accumulating on our eight pots of philodendron, but we did not know why it appeared or what it was. Some of our friends told us to water the plants from below, and some said to water from above. We didn't know why that should make any difference. Usually we allowed our eight pots of philodendron to sit in water all week long; we thought that was good for them. Poor philodendron—no wonder they perished! We had noticed that the soil on top became encrusted. We didn't know that anything should be done about it. In short, we knew nothing except that plants had to be watered.

Consequently, we looked for authoritative advice. In the library, we read book after book on indoor gardening which, rather than encourage us, confused us and gave us the feeling that if we had had prior courses in plant biology, general horticulture and perhaps one on plant physiology, we might better understand what we had been reading.

Amos Pettingill in his *The White Flower Farm Garden Book* says: "People just starting probably should not read garden books. At the early point in a gardener's life (or indoor amateur horticulturist's) books make gardening seem too hard. Garden books become important after a man decides he wants to know more. Then, they are essential."

Although we appreciate his comment and because of our own library experience confirm it, we feel that a beginner should not have to rely on trial and error until many years pass, many plants die and she builds a body of experience. The world loses too many amateur horticulturists that way. The beginner is entitled to definite guidelines that are not complicated; that answer her questions; that do not necessitate making individual plant nursing charts; that dispel timidity when she handles her plants; that make her confident and comfortable from the very start.

Therefore this book. It is a house-plant primer, an honest-to-goodness beginner's book. We remember one day in The Potting Shed when a customer said in exasperation, "I have a million garden books and not one answers my questions." No one needs a million garden books, but beginners surely need a book for beginners. A beginner's book must explain "why." A beginner's book must not suggest that the beginner use her judgment when without experience or knowledge there is no basis for judgment at all. It must foster the development of her judgment to the point where she will be able to say, "My experience tells me to do this differently from the way the book suggests." A book such as this will teach the beginner that her own experiences are as valuable as those she will read about. It will teach her to trust her own.

An honest-to-goodness beginner's book must promote

the confidence which immeasurably adds to the beginner's happiness in caring for her plants and is exactly why she has chosen to become a beginner.

We remember the winter a customer said, "When the world turns brown, I must have something green to live with." More fundamental is the growing realization that without plants we cannot live. Most of us understand that photosynthesis is the process by which plants using sunlight as the source of energy combine carbon dioxide and water to produce oxygen. Some of us realize that the total oxygen supply in our atmosphere is the product of plant activity. Ecology is no longer a word only for scientists. All of us are beginning to know that every organism is related to its environment and that the only way we can relate to this basic fact is through gardening. The burgeoning interest in house plants is one evidence of the growing awareness of these facts of life.

In preparing to write this book, we leaned heavily on our memory of what it is like to be a beginner horticulturist. We remember our painful trial-and-error years. We hope to aid you in avoiding this unnecessary experience. We shall answer the questions repeatedly asked by our customers because we feel they may be yours. In the section of this book called "What Is Your House Plant I.Q?" we shall list those questions. By the time you reach that section you will, we feel certain, be able fully to answer each question. And if you still flounder somewhat, you will be referred to the proper page in the text.

Judy, one of our customers said, "It is not enough to be told how to do something. We must be told why." Judy also said, "Putting a plant into a pot is a commitment. If you make that commitment you must give it a full measure of devotion." This does not mean an impossible list of things you must do. It does not mean tasks difficult to accomplish. It simply means that for you plants are more than inanimate, ornamental items in your house. Plants live and breathe, change and grow. They want you to observe them, touch them, love them and, given half a chance, with the beauty and joy they add to your home and to your lives, will return these gifts in full measure.

This book will also suggest a number of plants, small and large, with which you will succeed, from which you can make your first selection. It will suggest one or two reliable sources from which to buy. No materials will be suggested which are difficult to secure. Nothing will be complex. With this book you go comfortably and confidently on your way.

I

Know Thy Dwelling

TEMPERATURE

Know thyself, the philosophers teach. Just as important for the indoor gardener is the injunction: know thy dwelling. Your home will be your plants' home as well. Perhaps even before you acquire your first plant, you should take a fresh look at the three elements in your home environment which are essential from a plant's point of view: temperature, light, humidity. Plants depend, for instance, on a drop in temperature at night, the reason for which we shall explain later. Lighting requirements vary for different plants, but no plant can live in closet darkness. Central heating is cosy, but it robs the air of moisture. But the beginner need not be discouraged because a little forethought can take care of these problems.

The advent of central heating and the thermostat has made the control of indoor temperatures simple for human purposes. Many people leave their thermostats at a single setting all winter long and assume that throughout the house the temperature is fairly constant. But the fact is that temperatures vary considerably even in different parts of a single room, a fact simply verified by the use of a thermometer, a tool we think you should have.

This may be a headache for heating experts, but it is a

boon for indoor gardeners, because different plants need different temperatures at night. Somewhere in the room you can find suitable temperatures.

We are concerned only with nighttime temperatures since the normal range of indoor daytime temperatures is suitable for any plant—with the common-sense consideration that plants can't be broiled or frozen. Nighttime temperature must be at least 8 to 10 degrees lower than daytime temperature. Why? Because during the day the leaves of the plant manufacture food and only the lowered temperature at night enables the plant to circulate the food through the roots and all growing parts. Therefore, the crucial temperature for every plant is the nighttime temperature. During the night food manufacture does not go on but respiration—the rate of food using—continues. If night temperatures are too high, too great an amount of food will be respired and little or none available for growth.

In most houses, even with the thermostat set at a constant 70 degrees,* you will find lower night temperatures at the windows, in corners, and in different areas of the room. Heat radiating from electric lights is gone; minimal heat from the presence of people is gone; heat in the outside walls diminishes as the sun goes down. The combination of these factors produces the required nighttime temperature.

LIGHT

Light in varying degrees is essential because it is the source of energy a plant needs to enable it to manufacture carbohydrates. Many plants can live healthy lives in areas of lesser light or even markedly reduced light. You need to know what kinds of lighting your home can provide.

Consider first where your windows face. In the northern hemisphere the sun always moves in the southern half of the sky; so a window facing north won't get direct sun. An un-

---

* All temperatures are Fahrenheit.

obstructed southern window will admit direct sunlight all day long. An east window gets sun in the morning and a west window in the afternoon. Now consider whether anything outside blocks light from the windows. A south window obviously will not give a true southern exposure if a huge tree, high hill or neighboring wall is in the way. A south window may provide southern exposure during the winter when trees are bare, but yield only the equivalent of an eastern or western exposure during the summer when outdoor foliage puts the window in shade. Tall evergreens may block light all year around.

In an old house with thick walls, even the depth of the windowsills should be studied on a sunny day to see how much light is blocked from the sill and within the room.

These are factors which the beginner should take into account before she sallies out to a greenhouse. Then she can discuss with the greenhouse attendant the lighting she can provide before purchasing her plants.

A light meter, though not necessary at this point, will help to measure exactly the available light. The results can be quite interesting. A good instrument for the purpose is a General Electric nonphotographic light meter priced at about $30.00. A light meter measures illumination in footcandles. One footcandle is the amount of light one candle throws on a surface one foot away in an otherwise dark room. The following table will help translate the readings on your light meter into sunlight exposures:

> 8,000 to 4,000 footcandles—bright sun
> 3,000 to 1,000 footcandles—hazy or diffused sun
> 500 to 50 footcandles—light shade
> 15 to 20 footcandles will enable a plant to survive
> for a while.

HUMIDITY

As we've noted, centrally heated homes lack the humidity

plants must have to thrive. Even a furnace equipped with a humidifier won't supply enough moisture for healthy indoor plants. Arid air will dehydrate plants. There are a number of simple and inexpensive methods to remedy the situation. In a later chapter we shall explain these methods, what humidity is, and why plants need it.

II

What Tools and Materials You Will Need

In the care of your plants you will need to do several things:

Water
Fertilize
Mist
Pinch out
Prune
Clean
Stake
Repot

The first three—water, fertilize and mist—become your responsibility as soon as you become the owner of plants; the last five sometime after you have owned them. Consequently, we shall divide the routine care into "Before Purchasing Your Plants" and "After Purchasing Your Plants."

BEFORE PURCHASING YOUR PLANTS

Probably the day you become a plant owner and certainly the day after, you will have to water it. A pitcher can be just as effective for watering plants as a watering can. But if you have many plants grouped together, as we hope you will in order to create the effect of an indoor garden, the

29

long nose of a watering can will be valuable in preventing spillage. There are many sizes available in any garden center or hardware store.

According to our instructions, you will fertilize your plants once a week, so you will have sufficient time at this moment to read about fertilizing in the next chapter. There are a few things to tell you about fertilizers besides recommending that you use them. All we wish to say about fertilizers at this time is that they can be purchased at garden marts, most supermarkets and at Woolworth's.

It is important for the well-being of plants to increase humidity around them by spraying them and the surrounding air space with a fine drizzle. We call this misting or spraying. In the next chapter, we shall talk about humidity and why it is so important for plants. There are many kinds of misters on the market, plastic as well as metal, inexpensive as well as expensive. An inexpensive mister is the spraying nozzle which comes with aerosol bottles of window-cleaning liquids. Make certain that the bottle is well rinsed before you use it for misting. This type of misting nozzle suffices and can be replaced cheaply.

There is one special tool which we suggest you get, and we advise getting a good one. This is a tool for pruning. We suggest that you invest in a pair of sharp-nosed clippers—sharp-nosed to enable you to cut the stem or branch you are aiming for without causing damage to any other. We recommend a good pair because it will prove cheaper eventually by keeping its sharp cutting edge for a long time.

For pinching out, you *own* the tools you need—your thumb and forefinger.

AFTER PURCHASING YOUR PLANTS

In a later chapter you will read that one of the indispensable ways of keeping plants healthy is to keep them clean. For this, all you need is a kitchen sink, tepid water, and a soft cloth.

Stakes are needed to support plants that are growing

tall and cannot stand up without help. Stakes are slender bamboo sticks. They come in different sizes of length and thickness. Plant ties—with which to tie the plant to the stake— are made of wire with an insulating cover to protect the stem from becoming bruised. Also available is a plastic ribbon which comes in rolls. Later on, we shall tell you how to stake a plant.

For repotting, you need a plastic washbasin. We use one that is about twenty-one inches long, sixteen inches wide and about six inches deep. Across it we lay a two-by-four board approximately six inches longer than the length of our washbasin. We use it to rest the pot on. This is a neat method of repotting. Excess soil falls back into the basin as you fill the new pot. A satisfactory repotting technique will be described in a subsequent chapter.

Pots are sold in different sizes and in plastic, clay and pottery. We suggest that you buy only clay pots. Although plastic pots are becoming popular with many growers, we did not use them. Plastic pots reduce the frequency of watering because they retain moisture longer than clay pots do. But a clay pot enables you to become familiar with the typical drinking habit and drying out of your plant. Also, plastic pots do not allow the plant to breathe through the sides as clay pots do through their porous sides. Be certain there is a drainage hole in the bottom of the clay pot. Sometimes, by omission of the manufacturer, that outlined area is not punched through, and if you try to do it you may break the pot. When you have become thoroughly acquainted with the drinking habits of your plant, a plastic pot, if you insist on it, will not be harmul to the health and growth of your plant.

The shape of the pot is important. To begin your horticultural career, we advise avoiding decorative pots that narrow markedly from rim to base because they constrict the root mass. A plant that is potbound is different from the plant that has its root base markedly narrowed and thus, deformed.

Pots can, of course, be reused, but it is necessary to wash them thoroughly before they are used again. To re- move the white encrustation, the accumulated minerals, soak the pots either in a bleach like Clorox or in Lysol for about an hour. Then thoroughly scrub the pots and thor- oughly rinse them.

After telling you what we should about soil, we shall tell you not to use it; we shall advise you to put your plants into a growing medium which isn't soil as you know it from your garden. We shall talk about this in Chapter VI.

All that remains to say is that the above necessary sup- plies can be purchased at a garden mart or a hardware store when you need them. Except for the sprayer, pruning clip- pers and fertilizer, shopping for the other materials can wait. Right now, the first task is the pleasant one of selecting and bringing your plants home.

BRINGING THE PLANT HOME, AND INITIAL CARE

Every qualified greenhouse or florist will properly wrap your plant before allowing it to leave if the temperature outside is cold and unsuitable. If it is warm, wrapping is still necessary to protect the branches. If purchased in winter, in addition to its wrapping, it is wise to put the plant into the interior of the car during its ride home. Even when pur- chased in spring and summer, a ride in the open back of the car if the plant is not wrapped is inadvisable because wind will cause breakage and windburn. So, summer or winter, transport your plants home in the back seat of the car or in the trunk if the plants are small enough to allow the lid to be closed. Properly support smaller plants with wads of newspaper to keep them from toppling and support large plants with wads of newspaper plus empty cartons against which the main stem can be propped as it leans its length diagonally in the back of the car.

You have purchased plants for certain areas in your home. Smaller plants are designed for the window sills where light is most favorable. But your larger specimen plant is designed to beautify a far corner of your room where light is less favorable. You have been careful to describe the light in that corner to the greenhouse attendant and he has helped you select a plant which will thrive in that location. Nevertheless, do not put your specimen plant there when you first bring it home. It has come, let us say, from the optimum conditions of a greenhouse. True, it is a plant which did not need that amount of light to fare well. But it did get it and it became accustomed to it. You do not want your plant to register shock and drop bottom leaves when it is deprived of that amount of light. Therefore, it is wise to put this plant for a short time in an area where it will get approximately the amount of light it formerly received. Then, gradually move it toward the corner for which it was purchased. Let it stand in each new position for a day or two as you gradually move it back. You will find that this transition period will either completely prevent or greatly reduce the trauma every plant experiences in these circumstances with the result that bottom leaves turn yellow and drop off. During this transition period do not fertilize your plant. Fertilization is a spur to new growth and during the time a plant is adapting itself to new conditions you do not want to give it an additional burden.

What will you need for your large floor plants? Obviously, you need a saucer at least one inch larger in circumference than the bottom circumference of your plant's pot or tub. This is to contain excess water, because in a subsequent chapter on watering, we shall instruct you to water thoroughly. And if you water thoroughly, you will have water running out of your plant onto your floor or rug. Therefore, you need a saucer. Plastic saucers, unlike plastic pots, are recommended for this purpose because they are not porous. Thus, water will not ooze from the saucer onto your floor and damage it. It is not necessary to lift the large plant to empty the saucer. Use absorbent paper and let it soak up the excess.

Plant dollies with casters are rather expensive, but for

very large floor plants they make moving the plant for cleaning floor or rug or plant itself a great deal easier.

For your smaller plants you will need smaller saucers. However, smaller plants present the appearance of a windowsill garden only if they appear as a group. We suggest, therefore, that you invest a small amount of money in purchasing a tray of proper dimensions to fit your windowsill. Line the bottom of your tray with pebbles and place your plants directly upon the pebbles thereby dispensing with the need for saucers.

In purchasing trays, do not select those made of copper, brass or lead. When you fertilize plants, the fertilizing solution can release harmful compounds of those metals. Aluminum trays used in cooking often fit the required proportions and can be used. Plastic or fiberglass are also suitable materials for trays.

In the majority of apartments as well as in new houses, the windowsills are narrow. The depth of these sills is not sufficiently ample to permit more than a few very small plants. A minor architectural change will improve this. Take a thin board—plywood will do—the length of the inside measurement of the window and the depth whatever you desire to add and nail it securely to the window. The added room allows you to arrange a windowsill garden of luxurious proportions.

If you have a radiator directly under a window you are planning to decorate with a plant display, cover the top with a sheet of asbestos and put your pebble tray on top. Your window radiator garden will be quite safe.

Or place your plants in a pebble tray and support the tray on four end bricks on the radiator. The airspace between the radiator and the pebble tray will enable you to use that space for your plants.

III

The Why of a Few Necessary Things

What fertilizer shall you buy? There are many fertilizers on the market, some chemical and some organic. Some of them are soluble in water and are administered to the plant when it is watered, and some are in powder form which is sprinkled on the top soil of the plant. Some are in pill form, and are inserted into the soil. All have the three chemicals and trace minerals which are essential to plant health.

These essential chemicals are nitrogen, phosphorus and potash. The only difference among fertilizers will be that the amounts of these chemicals will vary. The numbers on the packages tell you the proportions of these three chemicals. For instance, if you see the numbers 20-20-20, you conclude that the fertilizer package bearing this formula contains equal and rather large proportions of the three chemicals.

The Brooklyn Botanical Gardens in one of their fine publications suggested 7-16-19 as an optimum balanced food for house plants. Fortunately, one of the most easily obtained commercial fertilizers, Hyponex, meets this formula.

These chemicals when administered to the plant function as follows: nitrogen produces good foliage and fresh shoots; phosphorus produces strong stems, root growth and abundant flowering; potash produces sturdy, compact growth by helping the plant assimilate its food.

Horticulturists advocate differing programs of fertilization. We experimented with daily programs but found no appreciable gain. We rejected the bimonthly and monthly programs of undiluted doses of fertilizer as too vigorous a thrust upon the plant. Finally we adopted a program of weekly fertilizing with a diluted solution and found this most acceptable.

Therefore, we advise that you use one-quarter of a teaspoon of Hyponex or a similarly proportioned fertilizer to one gallon of tepid water and fertilize every week. Fertilize throughout the year, except for the months of November and December. During these two months daylight hours are shortest and it is at this time that all plants need to rest. Fertilizer given at this time is unwelcome to the plant and will not be used. The plants have stored enough food to enable them to rest during November and December; they do not need additional food to keep themselves in very good health. You will notice that your plants will show no growth during this time but they will begin new growth about January. Prepare a gallon of fertilizer and keep it until it is used. Shake it well before using because the powder does not completely dissolve.

Resting and dormancy are two different things. A plant that is going dormant will lose all of its leaves and will be, to all appearances, dead. It needs to be put into a dry, fairly dark place and to be kept completely without water until new green growth is discernible. When this occurs, put the plant into a fresh, clean pot of the same size with fresh soil and begin to water it. Bring it forth into good light. A plant that is resting will keep its leaves but will be stationary.

WHAT IS HUMIDITY? WHY DOES EVERY PLANT NEED IT?

Humidity is the amount of water vapor in the air which surrounds a plant and directly affects the way in which it transpires. Transpiration is the way in which the leaves and stems of a plant give off water which then evaporates into the surrounding air. When the air surrounding a plant is dry, the plant gives off too much water and it may wilt when the water rapidly evaporates. But when the air is moist, both transpiration and evaporation slow down.

There must always be a balance between the amount of water taken in through the roots and the amount of water which the leaves and stems give off. If this balance is upset, the plant wilts. If your plant wilts too often, it will suffer serious cell damage. This is why you use your sprayer. With it you produce a fine mist of water vapor in the air directly around your plants as well as directly upon the leaves. Your plant will show its appreciation by its increased vitality.

There are a few simple ways of increasing humidity, and we have already mentioned three. We said that arranging your plants in groups enhances their combined effectiveness to create an indoor garden picture. Grouping also increases their ability to produce greater humidity because their combined transpiration increases the water vapor in the air around them.

The second method of increasing humidity is by misting with your sprayer. Although once a day is essential, if you have the time, it is beneficial to mist several times a day. Mist the leaves of the plant, especially on the undersides, and the airspace around them.

The third method is to group your plants on a tray lined with pebbles. Keep the water level in the tray itself below the surface of the pebbles so your plants do not sit in water. As it evaporates, the water in the tray will add water vapor to the air.

Fourth, if your plant is of moderate size and its position in the space it occupies allows you to raise it, place it on top of an upturned pot which itself sits in a saucer larger than the circumference of the rim of the upturned pot. Pour water into the saucer when you water your plant so that it will evaporate into the air and increase humidity around the plant.

If you prefer decorative pots, place your plant in its clay pot on any convex object inside the decorative container to insure that it does not sit in water, or use pebbles, and pack the space between the potted plant and the decorative container with damp, long-fiber sphagnum moss. Sand can be used for the packing, but it is more difficult to handle since you should remove your plant from the decorative container from time to time to empty any accumulated water. The damp sphagnum moss can be more easily removed and then replaced.

IV

How You Can Keep Your Plants Beautiful

When you purchase a plant, it is, we shall assume, in prime condition. It is potted in a good medium; it shows new growth; its color is deep green; and it has a lovely shape. It cannot remain in this condition without your help. Right now we shall devote ourselves to a discussion of the shape of the plant.

Branches of a plant do not grow in identical ways. Sometimes one branch juts out ahead of its companions. Sometimes one branch will lose more leaves than another. After a few months your plant has grown larger but it looks so different! Assymmetrical, perhaps? Thin and skimpy at the bottom? Or, if for a year or two you haven't done anything to insure its shapeliness, your beautiful plant has long branches which are bare except for a cluster of leaves at the tip. This condition is described as *leggy*, and when your plant is leggy it by no means is as lovely as it used to be; perhaps it is not lovely at all.

There are two ways by which you can keep your plant shapely and beautiful indefinitely. These are pinching out and pruning. Pinching out does not change the appearance of your plant. Pruning does. Pruning is a more drastic cutting-back process.

PINCHING OUT

Let us discuss pinching out. It is a process of taking the newest leaf bud about to unfold which looks like a tiny green spear, between your thumb and index finger and, using the fingernail of the thumb against the nail of the index finger like a cutting blade, cutting or pinching out the emerging leaf. Sometimes you will find this emerging leaf on the side of the stem near the tip and sometimes at its terminal point.

We always say "pinch out" after one of our friends, an intelligent person who had little experience and great timidity with plants, complained to us repeatedly that no matter how often she pinched her plants, they grew leggy and bare at the bottom. Finally, we asked her to show us how she did it. She gently pinched the emerging leaf bud but she left it intact on the stem! After that, whenever we explained pinching, we made certain to say "pinching *out*."

Sometimes pinching out may include more than the emerging leaf bud. It may have to include the last small cluster of leaves at the tip of the stem because without pinching out these leaves it is difficult to get at the newest leaf bud.

What does pinching out do? It produces new shoots at the base of your plant and encourages bottom branching. How does it do that? If we remove the tip of a stem, that stem for a space of time does not grow longer and no new leaves form on it. When the tip of the stem is present and producing leaves, it forms a hormone that moves down the main stem and prevents lateral buds from growing.

Lateral buds are present at every joint of the stem, just above the point at which each leaf is attached. These buds, like the very tip of the stem, have the capacity to develop stem tissue and new leaves.

If you want the lateral buds to develop into branches, simply remove the tip of the stem. A bushy plant is produced when lateral buds develop into side branches and when the tips of the stems of these branches are also removed.

PRUNING

Pruning is a more radical process. Here, with your good pair of clippers, you cut out dead stems at the base of a plant, cut back stems that are partially bare halfway up and you shape your plant according to your own aesthetic taste. Cut diagonally with a clean sharp cut and always cut close to the main stem if you are removing a branch, or close to the soil if you are cutting at the base. Shaping is an individual thing, a choice determined by whatever you desire.

Too many of our customers said they couldn't bear to pinch out or prune. From the intensity of their reluctance, they indicated that pinching out and pruning were destructive and did a disservice to the plant. But that is not so. *Not* doing it is a great disservice. Pinching out and pruning not only guarantee the loveliness and beauty but these techniques serve to prolong the life of the plant. There are some plants you cannot cut back. These are plants like the Norfolk Island pine (Araucaria excelsa) whose leader—the topmost branch—should never be cut. If it is, the plant continues to lengthen its side branches, but it will not grow taller and will lose its shape as a tree.

STAKING

What is staking? Staking a plant means to support it. When a plant grows tall and remains upright on a thick stem, obviously it does not need additional support. However, it is likely that all plants which grow up rather than bushily out from their sides and base need some support. Stakes are made of bamboo and come in different sizes and thicknesses. They are tied to the main stems with plant ties. There are varieties of commercial plant ties. The only thing you must remember if you are using a homemade tie is that commercial ties are insulated to protect a stem from being bruised. Select something that will provide the same insurance.

To stake a plant, insert the stake as close to the main stem as possible, pushing it deeply into the soil to the bottom of the pot. Do not worry that its passage through the soil may damage the roots. That may happen but this damage is slight and will not injure the plant. Then tie the stem to the stake with plant ties at the bottom and top of the stake.

REPOTTING

How can you tell when to repot? There is a great deal of questioning about when to repot as well as how to repot. How can you tell when? When your plant wants to be repotted, it will tell you in the following five significant ways:

1. When the size of a plant is incompatible aesthetically with the size of the pot—repot.
2. When a plant no longer can stand upright in its pot and falls over—repot.
3. When the top soil is no longer friable, no longer loose on top, when you can see and feel roots all over the top and when there doesn't seem to be any soil left that isn't hard and packed with roots—repot.
4. When water stands on top for a long time it is an indication that there is no air space left inside the pot—repot.
5. When water runs through immediately it is an indication that the roots closest to the sides of the pot have dried and died. The water then runs right outside of the root ball. When this happens—repot.

These conditions are the five which will indicate that repotting time has arrived. Roots protruding through the hole at the bottom of a pot do not indicate a need to put that plant into a larger pot; wherever there is an outlet, roots in a potted plant will protrude.

But don't be in a rush to repot except in the last two cases—numbers four and five. There is still plenty of time. Just remember that a potbound plant will take more time to water because the plant will use more water and the water will take more time to seep through the entire root mass of the plant. It does not hurt, if you remember the above, to keep any plant potbound. In fact, most houseplants will bloom only if they are potbound. Since it does not hurt to keep a plant potbound, you can experiment with a reluctant bloomer and see if it doesn't respond to potbound conditions.

A plant that needs to be repotted is to be put into the next-size-larger pot. The only exception to this rule is the plant that has been allowed to become and remain potbound so long that it will not fit into the next-size-larger pot without excessive cutting away of its root mass. Then it is reasonable to put it into a pot not more than two sizes larger. Otherwise, it is not advantageous to a plant to jump two or three sizes. Why? Because you will be putting your plant into too much soil which will need too much water for thorough wetting, and you may drown your plant.

How do you repot? Put the soil into the washbasin and moisten it. Law the two-by-four board across the basin. Put crock—a piece of broken clay pot—into the new clean pot, one size larger than the pot the plant presently occupies. Always place the crock in convex position to allow water to drain off. Crock is necessary so that soil does not fill the drainage hole and clog it.

In order to knock a plant out of its pot, follow this procedure: if it is a small-size pot, hold it in your left hand and invert it. With your right hand also supporting the pot, knock the rim sharply against the two-by-four board over the potting basin and keep your left hand ready to catch the plant as it falls out of the pot. If it falls into the basin, the falling distance is not great and no real harm will ensue. But leaves may be crushed; so try to prevent a fall by keeping the left hand alert. If the roots adhere to the sides of the pot, it will be more difficult to dislodge a plant. You may insert a dull table knife along the sides to detach the plant from these dried roots. Finally, however, the plant will yield to the impact of knocking and will be loosened from the sides. Cup your left hand, separating your fingers, thumb, index and middle fingers on one side of the main stem or crown, fourth and small fingers on the other side of the stem or crown. Cup your hand to hold the plant gently as it comes out of the pot.

If the plant is a large floor plant, lifting the pot and thumping it on a soft, firm surface will help to loosen the plant from the pot. Sometimes a very large plant, long pot-bound, is so adherent to the pot that it is necessary to break the pot to free the plant.

When the plant is out of the pot, you will find entwined, tightly massed roots encircling it. Gently untwine them and cut away those lengths of the root mass that now hang below the root ball. In a plant with very fine roots which seem to have completely used all the soil and has a firm mass of inter-laced roots, make shallow, perpendicular incisions with your clippers all around the root ball and gently remove that shallow section of root and soil between each incision. Also clip away a small portion of soil and root from the base. This will open up all side and bottom spaces for future growth of root. Do not be frightened. If your plant could talk to you, it would utter words of encouragement.

Now fill your new pot with about one inch of soil. We have said that you will not be using soil. You will be using a commercially produced potting medium which for brevity's sake, we shall call soil. Place the plant into the pot and look to see whether the plant when covered with soil up to the place on the stem previously reached by the soil, will leave a space at the top of the pot for watering purposes. If it does not, slice away another portion from the bottom. Pack the soil gently and firmly around the plant until you have reached the desired height. Take a bamboo stake or other suitable stick to tamp the soil down firmly along the sides of the pot to make certain that no empty spaces have been left at the sides. If empty side spaces are left, the roots will dry out and die when they reach into these spaces. Then hold the pot in both hands and thump it solidly on the board to settle the soil. Water it thoroughly until water drains out of the drainage hole because this will help settle the soil firmly around the plant.

Do not fertilize a plant immediately after repotting. It is best to wait for two or three weeks until the plant has again established itself. Some of the roots may have been damaged in the repotting process. If so, they will not be able to utilize the fertilizer. Instead, the fertilizer may burn the roots.

We never restricted ourselves to any special time of year for repotting plants. We repotted throughout the year whenever a plant indicated it was ready. Gently done, according to the above directions, no plant need suffer damage whether it is repotted in spring, summer, fall or winter.

If you pack the soil to the very brim of the pot, you will find it troublesome to water your plants. Water will run off before it can seep down, particularly in a potbound plant. Therefore, when you pot a plant or repot, always leave sufficient space at the top to hold enough water to insure a thorough watering for your plant.

The space that you leave for this purpose should be approximately two and one-half inches if you are using a fourteen-inch tub; approximately two inches if you are using a twelve-inch pot; approximately one and three-quarters of an inch for a ten-inch pot; one and one-half inches for an eight-inch pot and so on down the sizes. Approximately one-half inch will suffice for a three-inch pot. After repotting, it is wise to keep a plant for a few days in a location somewhat more shady than the light location it needs.

The vigorous growth of a plant occasionally becomes a matter of dismay because it becomes too large and no longer is suitable for any spot in your home. What do you do with it? Discard it? Of course not. You can keep a plant the size you want it to be indefinitely. This is how you do it:

Knock the plant out of its pot. If the plant is large, you will need help to do this. Both of you will lift the plant, one lifting the pot, the other holding the main stem and also gently tugging at it. Thump the plant several times on a semisoft, solid surface until you loosen the plant from the pot. You may use a dull knife to insert at the sides to loosen the clinging dried roots without fear of damaging the plant.

Then lay the plant gently on its side and with a sharp, clean knife, slice shallow, perpendicular portions from the sides, rolling the plant until you have sliced all around it.

Then slice a portion from the base—about one or two inches of it or even more. After you cut away a portion from the base, gently loosen all visible roots with a pencil or smooth, slender stick and cut these roots off. They are dried and no longer fulfill any function.

Lift the plant and put it into its old pot to see whether it will fit again once soil is replaced. If you think the root mass is still too large for the old-size pot, repeat the slicing process.

When you have trimmed the size of the root mass and the sides sufficiently, you are now ready to repot the plant. It is advisable, even though the plant has come from that pot or tub, to scrub it thoroughly before you use it again. Make certain that one of you holds the plant straight and upright while the other replaces and packs down the soil. Remember to tamp the soil firmly all around the sides. Remember also to water it thoroughly after repotting until water drains out of its drainage hole.

Now the plant is upright and you can trim the top structure. This is necessary because the root mass is much smaller and cannot nourish the plant in its original size. You must cut the plant back to make its top structure compatible with the root structure's ability to sustain it. Do not be afraid of cutting back too much. Shape it when you prune it according to your own aesthetic tastes. Now again, you have a plant whose size is comfortable for the space you planned for it originally in your home.

V

Even Beginners
Can Make Baskets

The beauty of the windowsill garden is enhanced significantly when a graceful, trailing plant potted in a basket hangs above it. Wire and plastic baskets are available in any garden center, and there are other ingenious devices currently sold which enable you to pot a plant and hang it. Pottery shops are making three-inch clay hanging jars with three small drainage holes at the bottom. But at this moment we shall confine ourselves to the more orthodox basket material.

The plastic basket is preferred by many people because it has an attached saucer and thereby seemingly obviates the necessity of removing the basket from its hanging wire and taking it to the sink for watering. This is of dubious advantage because the saucer is shallow and watering it in its hanging place, if the plant is watered thoroughly, will surely result in spillage. We did not use plastic hanging baskets for the same reasons that we rejected plastic pots. You will recall, we talked about that in Chapter II.

Wire baskets are more pleasing aesthetically to us. True, they will drip and they *should* drip when watered to indicate that they have been watered well. But you can choose a plant for your basket that will not have to be watered more than once a week. Surely then, it is not too much trouble to take

your lovely basket to the sink, immerse it in water for ten or
fifteen minutes until the top of the basket material is as wet as
the bottom and let it drain for a few minutes after you remove
it from the water before you replace it in your window. And
even if you choose a plant that has to be watered more frequently, aren't you beginning to be, like us, commited to the
idea that the few minutes devoted to a living thing of beauty
are not too much to spare?

You can buy wire baskets in many sizes—four and a half
inches, six inches, eight inches, ten inches and 12 inches. We
found that the majority of The Potting Shed customers preferred the six-inch size to others because it was more suitable
to the available space in their homes. We suggest that you
begin with a medium-size basket rather than a very small or a
large one. A very small basket may make it difficult for you to
manipulate the plant into it and a large-size basket can grow
to enormous proportions. A medium-size basket will give you
room enough—and not too much or too little—to practice
lining and filling the basket.

Now buy a package of sheet moss and one of coarse-
fiber sphagnum moss. Submerge each material in separate
containers and soak for ten or fifteen minutes until they are
thoroughly wet. Squeeze carefully to remove excess water.
Then line the wire basket with the sheet moss—moss side out—
leaving an overhang of about one inch at the top. Now, take
a handful of sphagnum moss at a time and fill about one-third
of the basket with the damp sphagnum moss, piling it higher
around the sides in order to leave a hollow in the center.
Knock your plant out of its clay pot and gently shake off whatever soil is readily removable. Place the plant into the hollow
of the basket and pack sphagnum moss around it until you
have reached the top of the basket. Make certain that you
have not left any hollow spots at the sides and pack the moss
firmly around the plant. Then take the overlapping inch of
sheet moss and pin it securely around the plant with fine hair-
pins. Attach the hanger to the wire basket and water the plant
thoroughly by immersing it in water. Let it drain and hang it

in your window. Now step back and revel in the exceptional beauty it contributes to your windowsill garden.

Pruning a basket plant is somewhat different from pruning a plant in its pot. When a plant grows densely over the sides of a basket—which is, of course, what you want—the top layers of the plant inevitably prevent light and air from reaching the layers underneath. The result is that underneath you will fnd brown, dead leaves. Then prune your plant in this manner and do it about every three or four months.

Turn your basket over and lift the sides of the plant. With your clippers, sheer away the greatest part of the brown and dead mass of leaves. You do not have to get every single dead leaf. Once the mass of dead leaves is gone, the rest will fall off. Avoid pulling because the dead leaves are intertwined with the green leaves growing above them and you will pull away masses of green leaves too. Be content with shearing the undersides of the plant. Then turn the basket right-side-up, let the sides of the plant fall down again and cut about one inch from the length of the stems. If there are any top stems that are bare, cut them back to their base. This will insure new growth at the top and center. If any dead leaves protrude through the green, of course gently remove by cutting them away.

A word of caution about the basket plant whose leaves and stems naturally entwine themselves as the plant grows. When you lift the hanging sides you will see such an intertwined mass of dead as well as live tendrils that it is impossible to separate the dead from the living. In these circumstances, be content with cutting an inch or two from the hanging parts of the plant. This will serve to spur your plant to new growth.

VI

Soil

Most people who think of putting a plant into a growing medium think of using garden soil. They think this is best because it is Nature's product, adequately and permanently provided for with nutrient content. This is an erroneous idea, however, for soil taken directly from fields and gardens does not prove successful for potted plants. Horticulturists now understand that the physical structure of a growing medium is far more important than its nutrient content. They think primarily of a medium which will hold the plant erect and which will aerate and drain well. The growing demand for plants which will thrive in pots and can be kept indoors throughout all seasons has spurred a search for growing mediums beside soil gathered from the garden.

Horticulturists also know that the soilless mix must be sterile—free of weeds, disease organisms, worms, and the like. An earthworm in your outdoor garden should be cherished because it performs an essential function: its crawling aerates the soil. But in a potted plant, a crawling earthworm separates the tiny hair roots of a plant from the soil, preventing them from fulfilling their function as feeding roots because, once separated from the soil, they dry out and die.

Sterilizing garden soil by baking it at the proper temperature in a home oven is a foul-smelling job. Our advice, therefore, to buy the commercially prepared product will be welcome to you. One of our customers resisted this advice and took earth from her garden compost pile for sterilization in her oven. Later she admitted that the mixture smelled so vile as it heated and permeated the entire house that it was impossible to remain inside. Moreover, her sister, having arrived during the process, said she could never forget the smell or be able to have dinner there again. Even the love of plants should not displace love of family.

For the people who persist in believing that soil, Nature's product, is best because it has Nature's own food in it, it is good to remind them that every time a plant potted in Nature's own product is watered, the food within it is leached out and eventually the cupboard within the pot is bare. Then you must provide additional food for the plant. Moreover, when you water a plant potted in the good earth, the water packs the soil so hard that it drives air out and the plant finds it difficult to breathe.

Many people also say that different plants want different soil combinations and they mix and stir and labor needlessly. But Andree Vilas Grabé said in her book, *A Picture Dictionary for the Home Gardener:* "Plants like people are remarkably adaptable and though one might prefer a woodsy soil, it gets along quite well in a not-so-woodsy soil. Plants have enormous tenacity and more often than not, can survive in the face of almost intolerable conditions."

Long years of research and experimentation have resulted in the manufacture of commercial potting mixtures that are sold in every garden mart and stores like Woolworth's. Some of these sterile mixtures are fine and airy and when water is added, the mixture will rise and will not readily absorb water. This is a condition easily remedied. Other materials added to the soilless mix make it absorbent. The best of the additives are coarse materials like perlite, vermiculite, sphagnum and sand. Perlite is volcanic ash and we preferred it. Sand is the kind that builders use—the fine grain—and can be purchased from a lumber yard.

We preferred perlite to vermiculite because perlite retains water on its surface while vermiculite collapses after a while. Sand adds substantial weight which makes it undesirable although for certain plants, as we shall tell you later, sand is necessary.

Sphagnum moss should be chopped or shredded into small pieces, and both perlite and sphagnum moss should be moist when added to the potting medium. The best way to moisten these materials is to pour hot water over them. Be careful not to touch these materials until they cool; they retain heat for a while. The sphagnum we recommend is the long-fiber kind, not the milled sphagnum moss, which is used in seed propagation.

The quantity of sphagnum moss or perlite that should be added is roughly one-third to two-thirds potting medium. This mixture can be used for every semitropical plant now cultivated as a house plant. For orchids and Bromeliads, osmunda fiber is best because it is a fern bark, wiry and tenacious, which clings fast to the shallow roots of these two plant families enabling them to stand erect.

We used the mixture described above for thousands of plants in The Potting Shed—plants of great variety—and we did it with complete success. There is one exception we wish to make. For a plant with a thick, heavy main stem like the Crassula which you know as the jade plant, whose main stem grows to a great diameter and whose leaves are thick and fleshy, making the entire top structure very heavy, the loose mixture we described cannot hold this plant erect. For this plant and others like it, we used fine builder's sand mixed with the potting medium in a fifty-fifty proportion. This mixture is firm enough to hold a Crassula and it drains and aerates very well.

Over and over again at The Potting Shed we were asked, "When do I water?" and "How much water do I give the plant?" We found that our customers wanted an arbitrary answer like, "Water three times a week," or "Water every day." But answers like these, although they relieve you of the responsibility of decision, will lead to disaster because they do not take into consideration variables like outdoor weather conditions which affect indoor conditions, the temperature you maintain in your home and the different drinking habits of a plant. But most important, they delay the development of your own judgment and discretion with regard to your plant.

For the question "How much water do I give each plant?" we shall ask you to be patient until you reach the chapter which follows. Right now, we want you to become familiar with your soilless mix and we shall, therefore, address ourselves to instructions which will be of great help when you yourself answer the question, "When do I water?"

How do you become familiar with your potting medium so that eventually your eye will become expert and you will be able to see at a glance how your plant is drinking and using the moisture you provide? The following advice is extremely useful in this process of becoming familiar:

Before you pot your plant, play with the soilless mix. Learn to know the feel of it and the look of it when it is totally dry. Then add enough water to moisten it. Play with it again until you know that feel and that look. Finally, soak it thoroughly and again play with it. Learn how it feels and looks when it is sopping wet.

This play period will be invaluable to you when you are learning how to water your plants because some of them want to stay wet, some want to remain moist, and some want a chance to become dry between waterings. The potting medium will easily tell you if you become familiar with it. You will be able to look at the plant and know what you have to do. You will be able to recognize at a glance when your plant is potted, the different stages of dry, moist and wet of the potting medium. For watering a plant is extremely easy if you take the trouble to know it and your potting medium. Watering is extremely important, but not by any means difficult to learn, if you approach it as a task you do with care and with patience. All of this brings us, then, to our next chapter— watering.

VII

Watering

It was difficult for us to comprehend why so many people found watering house plants a difficult problem to master until we remembered the first time we had to water the thousands of plants in The Potting Shed. We were told which plants required different degrees of wetness, but we were not able to tell what we had to do just by looking at the soil. Therefore, we had to shut off the hose in order to feel the soil and ponder a decision while we grew as soaked with anxious perspiration as our plants were with water.

No one need go through that painful experience. Nor is it necessary for someone to tell you the exact quantities of water to use. There is a far better and much easier way for you to become expert at watering your plants.

Every reputable greenhouse and mail-order house from whom you buy will give you the watering requirements for your plants. If you buy from the supermarkets, where very often not even the name is tagged, you must then identify your plant in order to learn it's watering requirements. It is much simpler to buy from a responsible greenhouse. When you have the essential information, how can you tell when you must water your plants?

In the chapter on soil, we advised some practice playing

54

with the soilless mix and we hope you took our advice and did it. Because, if you did, you now know what wet soil, moist soil and dry soil feel like and look like and you have the basic secret of that most important aspect of plant care—successful watering. For successful watering in the beginning is based on tactile information and there is nothing difficult about it. Let your fingers tell you. Place two fingers upon the soil and let them rest there for a moment or two until you can feel and recognize the degree of moisture still within the pot. You will be able to differentiate between dry and moist and between moist and wet. Eventually, you will be able to dispense with this tactile method because just by looking at the soilless mix you will recognize whether or not your plant, according to its needs, requires watering that day.

One of our customers translated the above suggestion to mean "poke your fingers into the soil." He succeeded in poking his forefinger into the soil to the depth of his second joint but found it impossible, he complained to us, to penetrate further. One never knows how one will be understood. You do not have to go poking your forefinger into your plant, breaking a few roots and possibly your finger. Just press your fingers on top of the soil and let them stay there for a few moments until they register a moisture reaction. If the soil is moist and sticks to your fingers, you will feel dampness and know there is moisture still within the pot. If the top soil is dry and crumbly and does not stick to your skin, there is no moisture left.

What does water do? It carries the food supply and enters the plant through the roots. Then it is exhaled or transpired through the stem and leaves. When you water thoroughly, the water redistributes the nutrients throughout the pot and enables the roots to reach out and grow. If you merely sprinkle, the roots turn upward, seeking moisture. If you water only one side, the root development is hampered.

One of our customers purchased a large kumqwat in magnificent condition; the ripe kumqwats hung on the tree in profusion. Several months later she brought it back. It was in pitiable condition. About one-third of the plant had died and the rest of it looked as if it would welcome a similar release. We examined it for disease and found none. We questioned what light and night temperature it had received and found both favorable. We thought it might have been attacked by some disease at its root but before unpotting it, we questioned how it had been watered. The answers solved the problem: the plant had been watered sparingly. It would be more correct to say that it had only been sprinkled each time it was watered. Concern for the expensive rug on which the plant stood was the prior consideration.

We also are concerned with expensive rugs and expensive flooring. But a plastic saucer of the right size would have saved both rug and plant.

We watered the kumqwat until water drained freely from the drainage hole and we were satisfied that the entire root mass had been saturated. It took an enormous quantity of water—from three to four gallons—the first time we watered it. Then we allowed the top soil to become slightly dry and repeated the process. In a few weeks the life cycle of the lovely kumqwat reversed from a slow dying to a slow resurgence of living. Its color deepened and finally one day it showed new growth. We had triumphed! Until it showed new growth, we did not fertilize.

When our customer arrived to take her plant home again, we questioned how much water the plant had been given. She had given it three cupfuls each day! Three cupfuls for a large plant in a twelve-inch pot and covered with fruit!

If we had removed the plant from its pot when it was returned to us, we would have found a parched, completely dry root mass. It is a testimonial to the plant's fierce determination to live that it survived such intolerable conditions.

A similar story concerns the customer who had an eight-foot-tall Dracaena marginata, a plant which wants to be wet all the time. Because the trunk of this plant which can grow to fifteen feet is unadorned except for the top where it produces a rosette of fleshy, linear leaves, our customer thought of adding some plants at the base to fill up what she considered an unlovely emptiness. This low-growing plant needed to become dry in the intervals between watering in contrast to the Dracaena, which needed to be kept wet. So she poured an amount of water daily into the center of the Dracaena, leaving the smaller plants around the Dracaena to become dry. This, of course, resulted in parching and distorting the peripheral root mass of the Dracaena as the roots struggled to reach the moisture in the center of the tub. Consequently, the plant lost many leaves.

We said that you must always leave a space in your pot for watering purposes, and we suggested approximate spaces for different-size pots. Fill the pot to the brim when you water and let the water seep into the plant. Fill the space again until water seeps from the drainage hole into the saucer. After five or ten minutes, empty the saucer. It is not beneficial to your plant to be allowed to stand in water. Plants must breathe, and one of their sources of air is through the drainage hole. Your plant will drown if permitted to stand indefinitely in water. If you cannot lift the plant because it is too heavy, soak up the excess water with paper towels. Never allow your plant to remain in water after ten or fifteen minutes. The exceptions to this rule are the plants which in their native habitats grow in bog conditions.

Many questions are asked about the value of watering plants by allowing them to soak up water from the bottom. It does not matter if you water from the top or the bottom except for the consideration that if you water consistently from the bottom, you will find salts appearing on the rim of the pot and the surface of the plant. This is the white granular substance that you have perhaps already noticed. When this occurs, you must water from the top to send the salts back where they belong.

Watering conditions change from summer heat to winter heat, but you are now knowledgeable and since you know by looking or by feeling the soil before you water, this difference presents no added difficulties for you. In the summer it is necessary to water more often particularly if your plants are outdoors, not only because of the hotter sun but also because of the drying winds. In winter you will find much less need for watering because of the number of dark, gloomy days. Finally, water your plants when the day's temperature is rising, not waning, and always use tepid water. Tepid water reduces the chance of leaf spotting. If you water as the heat of the day wanes, the leaves remain wet and become cold, thus increasing the danger of your plant's succumbing to a fungus disease.

What do you do if you have a plant that never seems to drink up its moisture and remains wet for abnormally long periods? Knock the plant out of its pot and examine the roots. If they are white and firm and there is no evidence of an unwelcome insect visitor enjoying the vitals of your plant, examine the drainage hole; soil may have blocked the vent. If the roots are dark and mushy and the soil smells sour, your plant has drowned and cannot be saved. Discard it. Now you have seen for yourself that the plant lover who knows that water benefits a plant and therefore thinks that a lot of water will benefit the plant even more, unwittingly condemns it to death. Be kind and loving to your plants, but transfer some of your kindness to restraint as your knowledgeable eye or fingers dictate the method you will use to water it.

When a plant is in bloom, even if it is a plant that needs to become dry between waterings, water more frequently. Do not keep it constantly moist, but do not allow it to become as dry as you would if it were not in bloom.

Now you have unraveled the secret of the green thumb which all plant lovers aspire to and foolishly envy in those people who have it and who, they believe, were born with it. No one is born with a green thumb. A green thumb is a matter of knowing a few basic things about a plant's culture— whether it likes to become dry between waterings; whether it likes to remain moist all the time; whether it likes to be wet all the time; what kind of light it needs to grow in or in what lesser light it can maintain itself; what degree of coolness or warmth it wants at night. A green thumb is only a dirty thumb or, more accurately, a dirty forefinger and middle finger, since it is easier to place these two fingers upon the soil than it is to place your thumb upon it.

There are some lucky insects which are able to grow appendages once they suffer a loss. But human beings are not totally deprived in that respect either. They can always grow green thumbs at any age, at any time. Green thumbs will just naturally sprout on people whose plants become an important part of their lives.

VIII

Do's and Don't's

The first precept under the Do's in this chapter is: Do feel comfortable with your plants. Since you have arrived at Chapter VIII, you now have a considerable body of knowledge and an incipient green thumb. You know the importance of some crucial things: night temperature and why it is important; light and how a plant uses it; humidity and what happens to a plant if there is an insufficient amount; fertilizers and what their numbers mean; and a whole host of things. So we can safely tell you to feel comfortable because plant care is no longer a mystery to you; you can feel secure that with your care they will thrive. It is of prime importance that you enjoy your plants. If you do, you will love them and the care of them will be transformed from an anxious chore to a relaxed pleasure. And only if you live comfortably with them, can you enjoy them.

Touch your plants. Not gingerly. Fondly and caressingly. Admire them aloud. Not only will all this benefit your plant, it will benefit you. It helps you relate to them. They live with you and need you and that is very comforting to know.

It is not a fantasy to think that plants appreciate your conversation. Dr. Edwin A. Menninger, who has made a study of the subject, reports that one Australian lady got remarkable growth in her garden as a result of violin concertos that she played to the plants every day. Dr. T. C. N. Singh, head of the Botany Department at Annamalai University in India, found a definite response by plants to music of the violin, flute and veena (an Indian stringed instrument). Plants assuredly do not know the difference between Bach and Debussy but they are stimulated to better growth by vibrations, by rhythmic sounds.

We have a Siamese cat whose name is Samantha. She is an important member of our household and a respected and beloved member of our family. She never pads into a room without a word or caress from one of us. She is a venerable ten-year-old who maintains excellent health. We know the in-gredients of her well-being are the conversations we have with her and the love we lavish upon her. In the same man-ner, your plants are important parts of your household, re-sponsive to your touch and voice. We do not imply that if you say a grouchy good morning to them instead of a cheerful one, they will know the difference. But we do mean definitely that they respond to vibrations emanating from you.

One day we found ourselves saying, "Whoops, sorry, didn't mean that," to one of our plants we had knocked over. We were vastly amused. But that's how much a living part of us they have become. If you are skeptical and do not believe that your plants like to be spoken to, and besides skeptical, if you are scientific and interested in research, a little time in the library will unearth proof of many experiments that prove that plants respond to touch and sound.

Another Do is: rotate your plants. Rotate not more than once a week. Plants are phototropic and will always lean toward their source of light. If you do not rotate, you will find in a few weeks that all the leaves will lean diagonally toward the windowpanes and away from you, depriving you of their full-faced beauty. That diagonal posture makes a pretty sight once you rotate your plant and it leans toward you. If you like the effect you may, of course, rotate less often and in-crease the angle. But rotate you must if you want a rounded growth. Wherever the light is, that is the direction to which the plant leans.

Now for a few Dont's: If the water you use is hard, the minerals leave a whitish substance on the plant leaves. You may for a special occasion want to spruce up your plant, shine its leaves and have it appear at its best. Plant polish is available at stores but ordinary milk—preferably skim milk—will serve this purpose as well. However, do not suffocate your plant in your attempt to glamorize it.

The breathing cells—or stomata—occur mainly on the underside of the leaf. If you cover them with a plant polish of any kind or with the milk you will make it impossible for the plant to breathe. Therefore, be careful that the material you use to shine the leaves is applied only to the top side of each leaf. Leaves that are suitable for shining are, of course, only smooth, leathery leaves. If the leaves of a plant are hirsute (hairy) or velvety, they cannot be shined. They can be well cleaned, however, by using a soft brush like an old-fashioned shaving brush.

When leaves curl, you may suspect that the plant is getting too much nitrogen. On a sunny day water two or three times to leach nitrogen.

Since plants breathe, you want to know how much air to provide for them. Plants use carbon dioxide as well as oxygen. Air must be present in the soil along with water for plants need oxygen at the roots. Plants therefore need a circulation of air which is easily achieved in every home in winter where doors are being opened and shut and in warmer weather where windows are kept open. What you must guard against is a cold blast of air blowing upon your plants. They will not profit by standing in a draft.

A circulation of the air in a room where your plants are will add to the humidity. Also, a circulation of air will reduce the possibility of fungus disease attacking them.

Plants adjust well to air-conditioned homes. However, it is important that you observe the reaction upon your plants of the air conditioner when you turn it on for the first time. Plants will dehydrate faster in this climate and will require more frequent watering. But they are better off in air-conditioned rooms than in uncooled areas during the summer months provided that the faster dehydration process is noted and taken care of. Professor A. F. DeWerth says that plants are superior when they are in air-conditioned areas rather than uncooled areas. The low humidity that prevails with air conditioning does not harm plants.

Do not water with ice-cold water. The sudden shock may cause leaf drop because the roots will not use ice-cold water. Always use water at room temperature.

Do not leave water in the saucer. After about ten or fifteen minutes, empty the saucer.

Do not fertilize when soil is completely dry. Water first with plain water. Then complete the watering process with the fertilizer water. If a plant is completely dry when fertilizer is administered, the fine hair roots may be burned.

Do not let the surface soil become encrusted. When that happens, use a household fork and loosen top soil.

Do not let your plants stand in drafts. They become chilled, lose moisture and will wilt; their lower leaves will become yellow and drop.

On icy nights, do not allow the leaves of your plants to rest on the frosted panes of the window. Protect them by propping a newspaper between the icy panes of glass and your plants—after you have finished reading the paper, of course. Or you may use a plastic sheet.

Why do leaves turn yellow? There are many reasons. It is natural for every plant to lose some leaves and produce new leaves. Some plants at certain definite periods will yellow and drop leaves from all its parts, not only from the bottom. These are soon replaced by new leaves. But when only the bottom leaves of a plant yellow and wither away, and when this process continues for an abnormally long time, check on the following possible causes:

1. You may not be watering thoroughly so that the entire root ball is receiving water. Correct this by watering over the entire surface of the plant until water seeps through.
2. Determine again whether the plant in question is one

that needs to approach a dry condition between waterings. Check that you are permitting this to occur. If you are not, the condition is caused by excessive watering.

3. Check whether the plant is standing in a draft.
4. Check whether the room the plant is in has undergone a sudden change of temperature.
5. Check whether the light requirements for the plant are satisfactory.
6. Check whether you have been fertilizing properly and properly means a regular program with stipulated amounts of fertilizer.

Plants protest air pollution by yellowing and losing their leaves. The same change can be noted when plants are exposed to fumes from artificial gas or paint. Natural gas does not affect plants.

A citrus plant whose leaves become yellow when they seem to be firm and healthy is possibly a plant that is in need of iron and is indicating an iron deficiency that can be remedied by using one-half teaspoon of Epsom salts and one teaspoon of sulfate of ammonia to a half gallon of water. Or you may use a teaspoon of vinegar to a half gallon of water. Or, if you can get aluminum sulfate, use one-quarter of a teaspoon to one quart of water. This does not mean, as one customer thought it meant, that you pour the entire half gallon of water on the poor plant at one time. It means preparing the mixture and using part of it when you water the plant, saving the rest of it for other waterings. Administer the mixture several times, one week apart.

Why are some flowers of the same plants brighter than others? This is only a question of a greater amount of light. Flowers which are pink in winter may very well become red in the summer sunshine.

Can you propagate cuttings in water? Yes, you can. Except for some plants, roots will develop in water. But water-developed roots are different from roots born in soil, and when a cutting propagated in water is transferred to soil, it may die. We found that propagation in sand, vermiculite or perlite produced vigorous roots. But we'll talk about propagation techniques in a later chapter.

What prevents plants from blooming again after once blooming? There may be several reasons: Use a fertilizer with a lower percentage of nitrogen. An excess of nitrogen will result in such a growth of leaves and shoots that flower production may be inhibited. Another possible cause may be lack of sufficient sunlight. Try intensifying light for an effect on flowering. Also try letting your plant stay potbound. Some plants will bloom only if they are potbound.

Some plants send forth their bloom only on new, terminal growth. If you prune this kind of plant at the wrong time, you are, of course, cutting off all possibility of blooming. You must become familiar with your plant's blooming pattern. If it is a plant that buds only on new growth, it is necessary to prune this plant frequently when it is young to insure bushy growth. Then, when this is achieved, let your plant put forth new growth, and it will bud.

When buds form and drop off without developing, it may be because you have rotated the plant and turned the buds away from the light. When buds form again, try not to change the position of the plant. Buds will drop if at any time in their formation the plant has been allowed to become dry. They will continue to form until they are ready to open but at the point of opening, they will drop. Therefore, a general conclusion can be made that any plant forming buds should never be allowed to become dry even if it is a plant which before blooming time desires to become dry between waterings.

At blooming time, check to see whether your plant is getting the required drop in night temperature. Also, when buds form, increase the humidity surrounding the plant. Mist more often.

Nitrogen stimulates foliage growth, but too much can retard the development of flower buds. Phosphorus, however, stimulates bloom. If your plant should have bloomed but has not, try administering small doses of phosphorus only instead of your usual fertilizer. Sometimes, too much potash will produce soft buds. If this happens, use a fertilizer with less potash.

A plant that can be divided has numerous shoots growing from the soil. Therefore, it can be cut in half because each half will have numerous stems, leaves and roots.

How do you keep a plant from getting leggy? Only a disciplined routine of pinching out and pruning will keep a plant shapely. Disciplining a plant in order to regulate its growth is as necessary as disciplining a child to insure its growth.

How do you make the flowers on a plant grow larger? By sacrificing some buds, pinching them off, the remaining buds become the beneficiaries of more food and energy and pay dividends by growing larger.

Why do plants grow in different directions? This question has already been answered. Just remember that plants will strive to reach the light. If overhead light is denied them, they will grow to the side, seeking it. You can regulate growing directions with the light you make available to your plant.

Should you follow suggestions in garden magazines? As a general rule I would say, "Don't believe everything you read." For example, we ruled out using peat pots for transplanted cuttings unless it was for a plant which grew unusually strong roots. At the time when a cutting is taken out of the propagating medium its newly formed, fragile roots are not strong enough to penetrate the peat pot as they grow. They will therefore be confined by the peat pot. Plants like Begonias produce tender roots, which do not have the strength to push through the peat pot.

Beginners are impatient and think a bigger pot makes a plant grow faster. Is that correct? No, it isn't. If you are an impatient beginner, learn that plants have their own timetable and you can't rush them. Indeed, put a plant into too large a pot and you will slow its growth. You might even cause its death by drowning—a fact which we explained in a previous section on repotting.

Why do you put crock instead of pebbles at the bottom

of the pot? Either one will do. The purpose of crock, which is a fragment of a clay pot or of a pebble, is to assist drainage by keeping the hole at the bottom of the pot from becoming soil-clogged. Therefore, either crock or pebble can be used. Just make certain that the pebble used is slightly larger than the vent to prevent its becoming tightly wedged into the drainage hole, thus defeating the purpose for which it is being used. Also, if you use crock, place it in convex postion over the drainage hole so that water seeps over its sides and out of the pot.

What is air-layering? Air-layering is a propagating technique which we shall discuss in detail in the chapter on propagation.

Can you use a milk carton for propagating? Yes, by all means. Cut the carton down and use it. It is not necessary to purchase special equipment. Any container into which you can punch a few bottom holes for drainage, and into which you can put damp material, is satisfactory.

How do you train a plant grown in a basket? Gently pull the stems downward and tie them with plant-ties to the metal parts of the basket. Do not tug hard at any branch. Pull them downward in stages. When a branch has become accustomed to its first tied position and maintains it when the tie is removed, gently pull it farther down and retie in its new position. Eventually, the branches can be untied and will remain in their extended hanging position.

What do you do when soil is washed out of a pot after repeated watering? Simply add more on top. Top-dressing plants reconditions them. Sometimes it is beneficial to dig out two to three inches of surface soil and replace with fresh material.

How do you make feeding simple? Prepare a gallon of fertilizer at a time—one-quarter fertilizer to a gallon of water. Save whatever is not used for the following week. Remember to shake it well before using if the fertilizer powder is not completely soluble.

When you have properly cared for a plant and, nevertheless, it is not doing well, what do you do? Knock it out of its pot and examine the roots. If they are mushy and smell sour, you have not taken care of the plant properly. The plant has been overwatered and nothing will restore it. Discard it. If the roots are white and appear to be vigorous, perhaps the drainage vent has become blocked. See to that. Look for evidence of insects. If you find none, look for any unusual growth on the roots. If you find a growth, you might try cutting it off and repotting the plant, but it would be wise to segregate that plant from all others. Watch it. If it continues to do badly, it might be well to get rid of it before it affects other plants. If you can find nothing to account for the plant's condition, repot it with fresh potting mixture, water it well and give it the best lighting conditions available. Stop feeding it until it seems completely recovered.

What clothes do you need for working with your plants? Old ones with plenty of pockets to hold clippers, plant-ties, etc. Never wear anything that you are reluctant to wipe your hands on.

What method can you use to differentiate watering needs besides grouping plants accordingly. A very simple method is to use different-colored plant sticks or different-colored plastic toothpicks. Print the watering legend on a piece of paper and tack it on some convenient wall so you will not forget that a red toothpick in the pot means wet; blue means moist; white means that the plant wishes to approach dryness. Eventually, you will know from memory and intimate association with your plants exactly what are the watering requirements of all of them.

Can you arrange leaves on a plant? Yes. In fact, you should. Leaves which overlap offer insects and fungi good breeding places. Gently—very gently—tug the leaves into spaces that are less occupied. This not only is a health provision; it is a method of adding to the beauty and symmetry of the plant. Occasionally you have to sacrifice a leaf if it persists in lying on another.

What do you do to carry plants through the winter? Adjust to the different watering conditions. The wet, sunless days will reduce the necessity of frequent watering. In your heated home, your plants will require more humidity. Give it to them by methods already described. Keep them clean. Fertilize them every week except during the months of November and December. If you have a long period of wet, gloomy, sunless weather, skip fertilizing for that period. If days are dull and dark, give them more light by leaving electric lights on during the day. Protect leaves from freezing on the windowpanes by suggestions already made.

What do you do when moss appears on top of the soil and algae appears on the pots. Scrape the moss off if it is just beginning to form. If there is a sizable amount of moss, repot. Moss growing on top is an indication that drainage is blocked or that the plant is too pot-bound. Wash algae off pots with a scouring pad. Neither moss nor algae will harm your plants.

Is there any general rule for the care of miniatures? One general rule is to reduce watering. Allow the miniature to become really dry, but not to remain dry between watering. This does not apply to bonsai.

Do you fertilize when light is inadequate? No, you do not. If you wish to or must keep a plant for a certain period in a light location which is not suitable, do not feed it. In addition, reduce watering. The plant will not grow in this situation, but it will resume growing when it is brought into suitable light. The plant's stored food supply will sustain it for a while. If you do try to promote growth while the plant stands in an inadequate light location, all you will get is a weak and pale growth.

What do you do when the plant falls over? That is either a plea from your plant to be put into a larger pot or a plea to be pruned. You can make your decision based on the shapeliness of the plant. If its shape pleases you, put it into a larger pot. If not, keep it in the same pot and prune it.

What should a beginner look for when she buys plants at supermarkets? Look for good, green color; for absence of insects; for full center growth; for emerging new stems. These plants are sold in plastic containers. When you get home, for safety's sake wash all the leaves well with tepid water (water at room temperature) and repot into the same size clay pot.

What should a beginner expect from plants ordered from mail-order houses? Shipped from a reputable house, plants will be well wrapped. Expect either a two-and-one-quarter-inch plastic pot or, at most, a two-and-one-half-inch pot. Unwrap the plant carefully and water immediately since the plants have been en route for several days. Usually, directions will accompany the plants. If so, carefully follow these directions. If no instruction sheet is included, it would be well worth your investment to make a small greenhouse for your plants by putting them into a tray and enclosing the tray securely with polyethylene material like Saran Wrap which permits light and air to enter and which will retain moisture. When you open your little greenhouse to water the plants, you will allow an adequate amount of air to circulate among them. Space the plants. Do not allow them to touch each other. Insert a stick at the four corners of your tray to keep the polyethylene from touching the plants. Keen them in their greenhouse for several weeks until they have forgotten their journey and seem to be acclimatizing themselves.

Mail-order houses will not ship in the hottest parts of the summer or the coldest parts of the winter unless you stipulate that you are willing to take a chance. But we suggest that you order in the most favorable periods of the year.

When moss in baskets is dry, how do you water? When the moss is dry and you pour water over the basket, the water will not penetrate the moss, but will run down over the sides. Very little water can penetrate dry moss when you pour over it. It will be necessary for you to remove the basket from its hanger and immerse it in the kitchen sink until it has absorbed sufficient water to become wet on top. Water must be tepid—not cold. When baskets are watered when they are still slightly moist, then they absorb water as it is poured over them. But they cannot do this when they are dry.

What plants like to be pot-bound? All plants like it. Some plants demand a pot-bound condition before they will flower. You are always safe to keep a plant in a pot-bound condition if you remember three things: water slowly and repeatedly until you are certain that you have watered thoroughly; feed in the same manner; water more frequently because the plant will dry more quickly.

What are the worms in the soil of house plants that wriggle in the water? These worms may be springtails or symphylan, a tiny centipede which feeds on the fine root hairs of a plant. For the springtails, use two to three drops of nicotine sulfate to one-quarter cup of warm water and flush the plant two or three times. For the symphylan, water the plant with limewater and repeat in ten days. Limewater may be purchased at drugstores, nicotine sulfate at a garden center or drugstore.

When do you pinch out and when do you prune? Pinch out when you do not want to alter the shape of the plant but you think it needs bottom growth to increase its bushiness; prune when you wish substantially to change and improve the plant's appearance.

What is grooming? Grooming is the whole process of pinching out, pruning, washing leaves, washing the pot, picking off dead leaves and other debris.

How do you keep your plants clean? Outdoors, fog, rain and dew help to keep plants clean. Indoors, cleanliness is maintained by washing both sides of the leaves once a month; by washing the outsides of the pot free of algae; by removing yellowed leaves, fallen leaves and flowers.

Why must you graduate the size of pots for cuttings and plants? Because of the danger of drowning your plant or cutting if you put them into an oversized pot. Also, you inhibit their growth if they do survive being overpotted.

IX

What You Should Do for Your Plants in the Summer

Plants benefit immeasurably in the summertime by vacationing outdoors. If you have a garden, porch or patio, you will find suitable light locations for all your plants. If you are an apartment dweller your plants will have to content themselves with the boon of air conditioning.

When they are outdoors, plants are washed clean by rain and dew. Plants that bear fruit, like the citrus and the pomegranate, will be visited by bees and pollinated. Air in greater amounts than is possible indoors will be available to your plants, producing the humidity they require.

The important factor is to remember the appropriate time for summer sojourning. Take your plants outdoors after the danger of the last frost is over. This period varies, naturally, in different areas. In the Delaware Valley area it arrives approximately by Memorial Day. In the cities it will come sooner.

When your plants are outdoors, you must be aware that they will dry out much faster than they do indoors; you will probably water every day. You may have to water some plants twice a day because of the drying effect of the wind. However, this last sentence is not instructional. You will still rely on your fingers and your eyes in judging the degree of moisture in the pot.

Since you are familiar with the light locations your plants need, you will place them in appropriate locations outdoors. Even plants like the Calamondin orange and the lemon, which rejoice in being placed in direct summer sunshine, will profit by a week's transition or hardening-off process during which time they are taken outdoors and placed in filtered sunshine, each day gradually moved toward their final destination under direct summer sunshine. A plant like the jade plant, the Crassula, with its thick, fleshy leaves, although able to take direct summer sunshine, will be scorched by it and therefore should be left permanently in filtered sunshine unless you like the browned, scorched appearance of the leaves. If you are in doubt about a plant, if you do not know its identity, place it in a very lightly shaded area and experiment with it as you move it gradually into a brighter light area.

The leaves of a tree make excellent filtering material and plants of the Begonia family, which thrive on filtered light will love their situation under the trees. You may hang Bromeliads in the trees where they simulate their native growing conditions. Ferns want the shelter and coolness of the trees.

Plants in hanging baskets will beautify your porch and there are many plants which will bloom profusely all summer long with just good light. Begonias are outstanding contributors to this kind of porch decoration.

Fuchsias make lovely hanging baskets. Until the weather becomes very hot and humid, let the fuchsia basket have filtered sunlight. With the advent of hot weather place the basket in an area which is light but more sheltered from the sun and cut the plant back approximately halfway. It will bloom once again in August and September. Fuchsias drink lots of water and require great quantities of air.

Just remember, water when needed. Do not follow any strict schedule like feeding the infant only at prescribed periods. The fashion has changed. Babies are nowadays fed on demand. For plants, the fashion has always been to water on demand.

If you want to insert your potted plants into the ground, do so—but only in their pots. If you remove them from their pots and plant them directly in the ground, the plant will do well. But if you hope to take it indoors in its original pot or even one slightly larger, you will have difficulty doing so. The roots of your plant will take full advantage of their unexpected freedom and will luxuriously stretch out into the soil far beyond the plant itself, becoming such a mass of lengthy root that you will not be able to confine it again in the original-size pot.

We wish to add a note of warning about sinking your potted plants into the ground. We do not advocate that practice because the sterile quality of the potting medium may be destroyed by soil pests which enter the pot either through the drainage hole or from above. We do not even advocate placing the pot directly on bare ground or grass. We suggest that you always put something under the pot—flagstone or board—to protect the plant.

However, if you insist on sinking your potted plant into the soil, prepare the hole and at the bottom put cinders to prevent slugs from entering the pot through the drainage vent. Slugs cannot crawl over sharp surfaces. Cinders will also help to prevent roots emerging from the drainage vent from entering the earth. If, however, that does happen, just cut those roots off when you lift the plant to take it indoors. One way to prevent roots from entering the earth is to lift and rotate the plant every two weeks. If roots have grown to the extent that you must cut six or more inches when you finally remove the plant from the ground, you will also have to trim the superstructure.

Now the summer is drawing to a close and you are expecting the first frost, which in the Delaware Valley occurs about mid-September. Take your plants in before that first frost. But before you take them in, put them through a careful physical examination. Examine them for evidence of pests. Don't forget to look at the sides of the pot, where slugs may cling, or at the drainage vent, where slugs love to curl up until nighttime, when they crawl up to the leaves and chew well-rounded holes in them. This is a good time to prune your plants or to pinch out. Finally, wash them thoroughly as an additional precaution against bringing any unwelcome pest inside.

Take your plants in before that first frost. In fact, if your house is becoming chilly in the mornings and you are thinking that any day now you will turn the heater on, bring all your plants in before you do so. The plants then will have a chance to adjust to indoor conditions which mean less air, less humidity, less light before you aggravate those conditions by turning on central heat. When you finally set your heater, remember to mist your plants more frequently for a while. The furnace will dry the air while your plants will still be adjusting to indoor conditions which are less favorable to them than the summer outdoor conditions.

As you did when you originally bought your plants, as you did when you took them outdoors, give them a transition period when you bring them indoors again. Put them in more favored light areas and gradually restore them to their original positions.

Your plants are now indoors and well adjusted and you are planning an early fall vacation. So, unfortunately, are some of your friends, to whom you might have entrusted the care of your plants while you are away. If you are deprived of a plant baby-sitter, make individual greenhouses for your plants, or group them together to make one larger one. In the larger group, prop stakes into your plants at intervals to keep the polyethylene (Saran-Wrap or something similar) with which you will cover your makeshift greenhouse from touching any of the leaves. Fasten the polyethylene to the stakes with staples or twine, draw it over the plants and tuck it in securely under the plants. This provides them with their own greenhouse. Before you cover them, water the plants well. Then your temporary greenhouse will keep enough moisture within the plants and sufficient humidity around them until you return.

A good greenhouse can be made in the bathtub if the bathroom has a window which allows sufficient light to enter. It can be a north window with strong, bright light. Sunlight is not necessary. Put your plants into the tub, water them thoroughly, and let them stand in water for about ten or fifteen minutes. Then drain the tub. Now cover the tub with polyethylene. Taller plants will have to have individual greenhouses constructed for them. This technique will keep your plants in good condition for two weeks at least. Do not do this for cacti and succulents. They can survive two-week periods without any attention. Of course, if you are planning an extensive trip around the world, this technique will not do. But yes, it will for a few weeks, and unquestionably it will for a long weekend. Go off and have a good time!

X

Some House Guests You Will Enjoy

Fortunately, the beginner who wishes to live with plants can now start with an exquisite collection, plants that are not fussy, temperamental and difficult, plants that are adaptable and not exacting, plants that from first acquaintance are a pleasure to offer one's home to. In this chapter we are going to suggest a number of these plants. For your guidance, so that you may quickly adjust yourself to life with them, we shall give you specific instructions for their care. We are going to tell you the temperature they were accustomed to in their native homes so you will be knowledgeable. But we are also going to tell you that although most of the plants listed in this section seem to want a night temperature of 50° to 55°F, it is definitely not necessary for you to turn your home into an igloo or deprive yourself of the pleasure of owning them.

We kept the large variety of plants in The Potting Shed at night temperatures between 58-60°F successfully in spite of their different preferences and at present in our plant room, we keep the night temperature at 55°F for a great variety of plants. Outdoors in summer our night temperatures do not go down to 55°F and certainly not to 40°F, the preference of some plants. Yet our plants forgot to be nostalgic for what they had at home and made the necessary adjustment. At the end of summer, they were in radiant condition, every one of

BEGONIA *'Silver Jewel'*

them. There is no reason why your plants will not adjust to higher nighttime temperatures in your home.

But we want to warn you that if you keep your home at 75°F night and day, your plants will not thrive and, we wager, neither will you. Far better to keep your thermostat at 70°F and throw a sweater around your shoulders. As we have explained in a previous chapter, the cooling house at night, particularly at the windows, will provide the required nighttime drop in temperature. Also, remember that plants have a terrific will to survive. They will do their share in accommodating themselves because of their ability to adapt to and tolerate the usual home conditions but they will refuse to do the impossible. Therefore, be reasonable and meet them halfway.

In spite of the fact that we have tried to be descriptively informative in the terms we used about watering, you may still ask: "What is really dry or crumbly dry?" But isn't it easy to tell the difference between wet which is a condition where you can actually feel water and moist where you can feel dampness? For the plants that need to consume all their moisture and become dry between waterings, here is a further guide for you: when you feel the top soil of such a plant and you imagine that you still feel some top dampness, wait until the next day to water it. A plant that needs this drying condition before it is watered again will never complain about waiting another day or even two days.

We refer to summer sunshine whenever we urge precautions against scorching or burning. Winter sunshine usually does not have this lethal strength although there are conditions where winter sunshine can build up excessive heat as, for instance, in a large bay window through which winter sun pours all day. It is the accumulated heat within this window area against which plants will revolt.

Since plants will become as dear to you as your other friends and you would find it unspeakably rude not to be able to pronounce your friends' names, we shall give you in parenthesis following each plant's botanical name, the correct pronunciation according to the diacritical markings.

BEGONIA MASONIANA, the 'Iron Cross Begonia'

The key to pronunciation follows:

a as in fat	e as in met	ō as in note
ā as in fate	ē as in mete	ö as in move
ä as in far	ē as in her	ô as in nor
â as in fall	i as in pin	u as in tub
ā as in fare	ī as in pine	ū as in mute
à as in Persia	o as in not	

The syllables to be accented are marked '.

We are dividing our suggested list of plants into the light categories: plants that will live and even bloom in areas of low light intensity; plants that need good light intensity but no sunshine; plants that need areas where they can get filtered sunshine—sunshine that is filtered either through a thin curtain or Venetian blinds and is not directly focused on the plant; plants that need unobstructed sunshine for at least four hours a day. In the low light category we shall pay special attention to the Pineapple family and in the filtered sunshine category we shall pay special attention to the Begonia family. You will find a glossary of terms used to describe plants on page 181.

Section of BEGONIA MASONIANA, the *'Iron Cross Begonia,'* showing the seersucker texture and the bold, brown-red pattern

Plants for Areas of Filtered Sunshine

BEGONIAS

One species of plant particularly suitable for home growing and blooming is the versatile Begonia. In this family there are miniatures with tiny leaves, giants that grow six feet tall, uprights, creepers and crawlers. Thousands of varieties provide an infinite range of color, texture and shape of leaf. Begonia flowers thrust themselves high above the leaves in spectacular branching clusters, or hang pendant in colors ranging from white to fiery orange and red. The texture of the leaves varies from sheerest silk, taffeta and velvet to tweed, velour and puckered seersucker.

Beginners are always keen to have their plants come into bloom, and the Begonia is willing to please. If the proper selection is made, you can have a Begonia in bloom for every month of the year, it is on this basis that our selections for you have been made.

Consideration also has been taken of the size of the begonias selected. They will be classified as begonias to be grown on windowsills and begonias that grow upright so large that they can be used spectacularly alone as specimen plants exhibited on a stand near the window, or even large enough to stand on the floor itself.

83

ACORUS GRAMINEUS VARIEGATUS, *'Chinese Sweet Flag'*

We shall designate the watering needs of each variety by using the letters "M," "W" and "D" which will mean moist, wet and dry. Remember that "dry" means *approach* dryness, not *remain* dry. The night temperature for begonias can safely be 62 to 65 degrees. Our method of classification will also separate Begonias into their blooming periods. Pronunciation will be given at the end of the chapter.

SPECIMEN PLANT	BLOOMING TIME	WINDOW SILL
'Black Falcon' (M)	January	'Gaytime ' (M)
'Joe Hayden' (W)	"	'Bow-nigra' (M)
'Bessie Buxton' (M)	"	'Cleopatra' (M)
x erythrophylla 'helix' (M)	"	
'Verde Grande' (M)	"	
scharffii (D)	February	'Tea Rose' (M)
'Alzasco' (M)	"	'Bobolink' (M)
'Dorothy Barton' (D)	"	
'Esther Albertine' (D)	"	
'Fischer's ricinifolia' (M)	"	
'Rosea gigantea' (M)	"	
'Mrs. Fred D. Scripps' (M)	"	
heracleifolia (M)	"	
Gwen Lowell (D)	March	'Leslie Lynn' (D)
'Ricky Loving' (W)	and	macrocarpa (D)
'Ricky Minter' (M)	April	'Sachsen' (D)
'Orange-Rubra' (D)	"	Helen W. King (M)
'Rubaiyat' (D)	"	'Anna Christine' (D)
		epipsila (M)
Jill Adair (D)	May	undulata 'Perfecti-
Orangeade (D)	and	flora' (M)
Jeanne Fleetham (D)	June	Frances Lyons (D)
Lenore Olivier (D)	"	x margaritae (M)

AMOMUM CARDAMON, *'Ginger Plant'*

Flamingo (M)	July	sanguinea (M)
B. acutifolia (M)	and	Missouri (M)
'Corallina' (M)	August	'Silver Jewel' (M)
B. minor (M)	"	
B. venosa (M)	"	
B. luxurians (M)	"	
masoniana (M)	"	
dierna (D)	September	metallica (M)
Esther Albertine (D)	"	obscura (M)
rex 'Fireflush' (M)	"	
Laura Engelbert (D)	"	
Sophie Cecile (D)	October	semperflorens— cucullata var. hookeri (D)
scharffii (D)	November	'Silver Jewel' (M)
	and	'Preusen' (D)
	December	'crispie' (M)

BEGONIAS THAT BLOOM INTERMITTENTLY THROUGHOUT THE YEAR:

schmidtiana (D)
Anna Christine (D)
Rieger Begonia (M)
Di-Shasta (D)
'Orange-Rubra' (D)
'Rubaiyat' (D)
'Preusen' (D)
'Lulu Bower' (D)
semperflorens var. (D)

Rex begonias want more shade than their kindred. They do not like to be in direct sunlight. These are plants which flower shyly; their flowers hide behind the leaves. But the

CYPERUS DIFFUSUS, *'Umbrella Tree'*

exquisite coloring of the leaves dwarfs the beauty of the flowers. You can select Rex begonias where silver is the dominant color; where the brilliant colors include pink, mottled rose and silver, deep plum, taffeta silver overlaid with blush pink, rose on black, green with chocolate brown markings, red and brilliant green, green leaves—black-veined. The list of color combinations could continue endlessly.

At the present time in our home we have Rex begonia 'Fireflush' magnificently decorating the deep windowsill of our bathroom. Its leaves are light green, edged with a deep red which looks black. The veins are red and the entire leaf is covered with red hairs. The petioles are red. The emerging leaf looks like velvet. It is blooming now, and although it is gratifying always to see our plant in bloom, it is the leaves which are so exciting!

The following list includes some of the Rex Begonias which we grew in The Potting Shed and which we brought into our home at various times to live there with us. All rexes want to be moist—not wet, moist. Protect them from sun if you must use a southern window. An east or west window is preferred. Since you will not be concerned primarily with their blooming time, the list is divided according to the size they can grow and a short description is added.

SPECIMEN

rex *'Fireflush'* —already described

rex *'Silver King'* —large, steel grey leaf

rex *'Helen Teupel'* — garnet brushed with silver

rex *'Princess of Hanover'* — green with tiny light pink hairs

WINDOWSILL

rex *'Merry Christmas'* — satiny red outlined in bright green with velvety red center

rex *'Can-Can'* —taffeta silver overlaid with blush pink

rex *'Dew-Drop'* —matte silver above, maroon underside

DIZYGOTHECA ELEGANTISSIMA, *'False Aralia'*

rex *'Emerald Giant'* —
green and brown
rex *'Stardust'* —large,
dark olive—green dusted
with silver

rex *'Baby Rainbow'* —
green leaves with purple
center, purplish brown
and carmine red
margins, silver spotted

Even when a Begonia is listed as one which appreciates the opportunity to become dry between waterings, when it is in bloom it is wise to water it before it becomes dry.

It is difficult not to use superlatives when describing begonias. In our plant room at this present time (November) we have Begonia masoniana, the *'Iron Cross'* Begonia sitting on a pedestal. Its leaves are almost twelve inches across, round, firm and seersuckered. Bands in the shape of a cross are brownish red. As the leaves grow older, they are overlaid with silver and covered with bristly red hair. Although it is supposed to bloom from either May or perhaps June to August, our masoniana blooms through November.

Beside it on its own pedestal is Begonia scharffii, which blooms through the winter, sending clusters of large, hirsute, pink flower clusters above the heart-shaped, olive green, hairy, toothed leaves.

On the shelf Begonia 'Anna Christine' is a dark contrast with its red pendant flower clusters and dark green leaves. On the same shelf Begonia 'Esther Albertine' presents such an abundance of pink flowers that the light green leaves seem to float in a bower of bloom.

Begonias are easy to grow, undemanding in their needs and seem so appreciative of the little care they require and get that they repay in more than double measure. Walk into a room with blooming begonias on a dull, dark and dreary winter day and they will transform it.

FATSIA JAPONICA

PRONUNCIATION FOR BEGONIAS

x erythrophylla 'helix' (ĕr–i–thrō–fī–la hē'–lix)
Verde Grande (ver–di)
scharffii (shär'–fē)
Fischer's ricinifolia (rī–sin–i–fō'–li–a)
Rosea gigantea (rōz'–ē–a gī–gan–tē'–a)
heracleifolia (her–a–kle–fō'–lē–a)
B. acutifllia (a–kū–te–fō'–lē–a)
masoniana (ma–sō–nē–a'–na)
Dierna dī–ēr'–na)
macrocarpa (mak–rō–kär'–pa)
Sachsen (sak–sen)
epipsila (e–pip'–si–la)
undulata Perfectiflora (un–dū–lä–tä per–fek–ti–flō'ra)
x margaritae (mär–ga–rē–'tī)
sanguinea (san–gwin'–ē–a)
Mettalica (me–tal'–i–kä)
semperflorens cucullata va. hookeri
    (sem–per–flō–'renz   kū–kū–lä'–tä)
Preusen (proi'–sen)
schmidtiana (schmid–tē–a'–na)
Di-Shasta (dī–shas'–ta)
rex Helen Teupel (toi–pel)

Section of FATSIA JAPONICA showing the broad, lobed leaf, with the veins radiating from the tip of the petiole

Areas of Filtered Sunshine

ACORUS GRAMINEUS VARIEGATUS (ak'–ō–rus gra min'–
ē–us vär–i–e–gā'–tus) comes from China and Japan and is
called 'Chinese Sweet Flag.' It wants to be kept wet, in
nighttime temperature of 40 to 45 degrees and in filtered
sunshine. (Don't forget what we said about the adaptability
of plants. We have a beautiful Acorus in our plant room
which does not remotely reach 45 degrees at night and
it has been beautifully healthy for almost four years.) It
has creeping rhizomes and tufted linear, flat leathery
leaves, light green and white, spreading fanlike.
See page 84.

AMOMUM CARDAMON (am'–ō–mum cär'–dà–mon) comes
from Java and is called 'Ginger Plant' because its leaves
when rubbed give off a spicy aroma. It wants a night
temperature of 62 to 65 degrees. It wants to be kept
moist in filtered sunlight, although a good light without
sunshine seems to keep it in fine condition. It is a durable foliage plant and will grow two feet high. It has
linear-lanceolate, leathery leaves, deep dull green in
color. See page 86.

95

FICUS PUMILA MINIMA growing on driftwood, 'Creeping Fig'

AUCUBA JAPONICA VARIEGATA (â–kū′–ba ja–pon′–i–ka vãr–i–e–gā′–tâ) is called the 'Gold Dust Tree' and is found from the Himalayas to Japan. It can take cold night temperatures down to 40 to 45 degrees, but like the others it will adapt itself to warmer nights. Dark green blotched with yellow leaves are opposite, shining, leathery and elliptic. The upper halves are toothed. Purple flowers appear at the base and female plants produce scarlet berries. The Aucuba wants to become dry between waterings. Feel the soil. When it is crumbly and does not adhere to your fingers, water thoroughly. Keep it in filtered sunshine or strong light.

CHLOROPHYTUM CAPENSE (klō–rō–fī′–tum kà–pens′) is called the 'Spider Plant' because it sends out runners which bear young plants. This name, however, is most unfortunate, for it is an intriguing plant. Excellent either for a hanging pot or basket it is a delightful, airy trailer. If it is neglected for a short time it will not sulk; you may depend upon it to take care of itself. It comes from Africa, wants a 50 to 55 degree night temperature, filtered sunlight or good light and needs to be kept moist. It is glaucous, has narrow concave leaves with parallel veins and long, branched raceme with small white flowers.

CYPERUS DIFFUSUS (sī–pē′–rus di–fū′–sus) is an extremely satisfactory plant. It comes from Mauritius, an island east of Madagascar. It is a compact, bushy plant with sturdy, three-angled stalks with a crown of broad, matte green, rough leaves and long, pale brown spikelets. This plant is so easily divided and becomes bushy again so quickly that it is an excellent source of plant gifts for your friends. It wants a night temperature of 50 to 55 degrees filtered sunshine and needs to be kept wet. *See page 88.*

DIZYGOTHECA ELEGANTISSIMA (di–zi–gō–thē′–ka el–e–gan–tis′–i–mä) deserves its name for it is truly an elegant plant.

HELXINE SOLEIROLII, *'Baby's Tears'*

One can become lyrical in describing its airy grace, which one often finds in an Oriental painting. Like a tree against the sky, its loveliness can be seen most vividly against a white wall. The threadlike narrow segments of the leaves are metallic, red brown and lobed. The slender stem is a mottled cream color. It forms a small tree and can grow to twenty-five feet high but can be kept shorter by nipping out the newest growth. It wants a night temperature of 62 to 65 degrees and needs to be moist. By all means, keep this plant just moist, not wet. *See page 90.*

FATSIA JAPONICA (fat'–si–a ja–pon'–i–ka) comes from Japan. It is an evergreen shrub with milky white flowers. The leaves are leathery, palmately and broadly lobed, dark shining green. The lobes are pointed and toothed. It wants to be kept moist in an area of filtered sunlight, and its night temperature can do down to 40 degrees. *See page 92.*

FICUS PUMILA (fī'–kus pū'–mi–lä) is a member of the fig family but altogether different in size from its relatives Ficus benjamina, Ficus retusa or Ficus decora. It comes from China, Japan and Australia and is called the 'creeping fig' because it is a freely branching creeper. The leaves are small, obliquely cordate, dark green, less than one inch long. It clings tenaciously to any surface. It appreciates filtered sunlight, a 62- to 65-degree night temperature and needs to be kept moist. *See page 96.*

HELXINE SOLEIROLII (hel–zī'–nē sō–lī'–rō–lī) has a charming common name of 'Baby's Tears.' It is also known as 'Mother of Thousands.' It grows low like moss and forms dense mats over pots. It has tiny green leaves and intertwining branches. Keep it wet all the time. This plant can be set in water and kept in water all the time where it grows nicely. It wants a filtered sunlight or good light and a night temperature of 50 to 55 degrees. *See page 98.*

PANDANUS VEITCHII, 'Screw Pine'

PANDANUS VEITCHII (pan–dān'–us vēch'–i–ī) comes from Polynesia and is called 'Screw Pine' because the leaves recurve into spirals. It wants to be allowed to become crumbly dry between waterings and it appreciates filtered sunshine or good light without sun and a 62- to 65-degree night temperature. Full-grown it is a stately plant. The leaves are wide and narrow to a fine point, light to deep green, lined and margined with creamy white. Small spines edge the leaves. *See page 100.*

SCHLUMBERGERA BRIDGESII (schlum–bēr'–je–rä bri–jēs'–i–ī) comes from Brazil; you probably know it as the 'Christmas Cactus.' It branches with small, glossy green, leaflike joints, crenate and with pendant flowers and flaring petals which are carmine red tinged with purple in the center. It wants a night temperature of 62 to 65 degrees, filtered sunshine, and while it is blooming it needs to be moist. After its blooming, let it become crumbly dry between waterings.

TOLMIEA MENZIESII (tol–mē'–a men–zi–ē'–zi–ī) is found from Alaska down to the coast of California. It is called the 'Piggyback plant' because new plantlets ride the backs of mature leaves, growing out of their base. It wants good light or filtered sunlight and a night temperature from 40 to 55 degrees. Keep it moist. The leaves are soft-lobed, toothed and fresh green in color.
See pages 102 and 103.

TOLMIEA MENZIESII, *'Piggy-back Plant,'* *'Mother of Thousands'*

Plants Which Grow Well
in Low Light Intensity

Plants suggested in this section do not need any sunshine at all. Some of them can survive even in a dim light. These plants all have broad leaves or lots of leaves which enable them to take advantage of all available light. We have experimented by keeping plants in this category in windowless rooms under artificial light of a low intensity of fifteen to twenty footcandles and the plants remained in good condition. Do you remember that we said one footcandle is the amount of light cast by a candle in a dark room on a surface one foot away? Remember this and you can visualize the low amount of light with which these plants can maintain themselves.

We said in the paragraph above that plants can *maintain themselves* in such a light. We did not say *grow*.

In order for plants in this category to grow, there must be light coming in from a window, or the plant must have more light intensity from artificial sources. These plants and all others benefit enormously if they can be taken outdoors into bright light or even well-filtered sunlight. They will store up quantities of energy which they will use when they are again returned indoors to an area of low light intensity.

We would like to caution you about the use of water and

Section of TOLMIEA MENZIESII showing soft, lobed and toothed leaves with young plantlets growing from the base of mature leaves

fertilizer for all plants placed in areas of low light intensity. Even where we list a plant as wishing to be kept moist, cut back on watering as long as the plant is kept in dim light. Let the plant approach dryness between waterings. Also, cut down on fertilizing to twice a year. Water and fertilizer prod a plant to grow. But without better light, the plant cannot comply. Adequate light is the force which enables a plant to utilize water and fertilizer.

If possible, when you keep plants for long periods in areas of low light intensity and cannot take them outdoors or even move them to a window at intervals, let a 100-watt bulb from an overhead bridge lamp shine on your plant for periods of four to five hours. In this situation you can slightly increase the water and fertilizing.

The following suggested plants meet the above conditions, enhance the beauty of your home and are easy to care for:

AGLAONEMA ROEBELINII (ag–la–ō–nē'–ma rō–be–lē'–ni) comes from Malaya and Borneo and is called 'Chinese Evergreen.' It has large, ovate, pointed leathery, grayish green leaves variegated with silver. It does not need sun and will do well in a minimum light. Keep it moist and give it a 62- to 65-degree night temperature. There are many different varieties. All of them are suited to this area of minimum light. *See page 108.*

ARAUCARIA EXCELSA (âr-a-ká–ri-à ex sel'–sä) comes from the South Pacific and is called 'Norfolk Island pine.' It will do very well in a shady northern light. It is shaped like a Christmas tree and can be used for that purpose by decorating it with small, light ornaments. Its tiers of branches are parallel to the ground. The awl-shaped needles are soft and bright green. It wants to be kept moist in a night temperature of 50 to 55 degrees. Do not prune this plant. If its leading branch is cut, it will not grow taller, and it will eventually lose its treelike shape. *See page 106.*

ARAUCARIA EXCELSA, 'Norfolk Island Pine'

ASPIDISTRA ELATIOR (as–pi–dis'–trà ē–là'–ti–ôr) comes from China and because it has tough, leathery foliage with shining, blackish green, oblong leaves growing from the base and thick roots, it is called the 'Cast Iron Plant.' It is most undemanding and almost indestructible. The leaves grow to about two and one-half feet long and they narrow to a channeled stalk. Aspidistra produces bell-shaped flowers at the surface of the ground. It needs no sun. It wants to be moist and cool at night, 50 to 55 degrees.

CISSUS RHOMBIFOLIA (sis'–us rom–bi–fō–li–a) comes from the West Indies and South America and its common name is 'Grape Ivy.' It is an excellent house plant for shady areas. It is a scandent plant with brown, hairy branches and coiling tendrils. Its leaves are thin and fleshy, wavy-toothed, with a glabrous surface, fresh green to metallic deep green. It wants a night temperature between 50 and 65 degrees, and it wants to be given a chance to become slightly dry between waterings. Placed on a high place like a mantelpiece it both arches its tendrils high against the wall or trails them in graceful, hanging beauty. *See page 112.*

DIEFFENBACHIA AMOENA (dēf–en–bak'–i–a a–mēn'–a) comes from Costa Rica and Colombia. It is a sturdy, thick-stemmed plant with large, pointed, oblong, glabrous leaves. They are deep green and are marked with cream white bands and blotches. Dieffenbachia grows tall and can be used imposingly alone to beautify a corner. It wants a night temperature of 62 to 65 degrees. Let it become really dry between waterings. *See page 110.*

DRACAENA GODSEFFIANA (drà–sē'–na god–sef–fī–an'–à) comes from the Congo and Guinea. It is a small, shrubby plant with wiry stems. The leaves are thin and leathery, elliptic, in whorls of three, glossy, deep green, irregularly

AGLAONEMA 'PSEUDO-BRACTEATUM, *'Golden Aglaonema'*

spotted with yellow. The flowers are greenish yellow and are followed by red berries. It wants a night temperature of 62 to 65 degrees and it must be kept wet. There are other varieties of small, shrubby Dracaenas, all of them good for the home.

DRACAENA MARGINATA (dra–sē'–na mär–ji–nā'–ta) comes from Madagascar. This is a tall plant of dramatic, exotic posture. It grows to a grand height of ten feet with a terminal rosette of dense, thick, fleshy, narrow linear leaves about fifteen inches long, spreading horizontally. The color of the leaves is deep olive green edged in red. It is a fine, durable plant which captures the eye and holds it. In winter give it a little more light, perhaps with some artificial lighting. It wants a night temperature of 62 to 65 degrees and needs to be kept wet.
See page 114.

FICUS BENJAMINA (fī–kus ben–jä–mīn'–à) comes from India and Malaya. Its lovely, romantic name of 'Weeping Fig' is fitting because it grows into a tree of dense growth; its branches droop; its leaves shine deep green, long ovate, slender pointed, four to six inches long. There is no corner of your home more graciously enhanced than by this appealingly beautiful plant. It wants a night temperature of 62 to 65 degrees and needs to be kept evenly moist. *See page 118.*

FICUS RETUSA (fī'–kus rē–tūs'–a) is another member of the fig family. It comes from Malaya and is given the enchanting name of 'Indian Laurel.' It is glabrous, and unlike its relative, Ficus benjamina, its branches are erect. The leaves are elliptic, small and rubbery about three inches long, green and smooth. It wants a night temperature of 62 to 65 degrees and needs to be kept moist.

DIEFFENBACHIA AMOENA, *'Giant Dumb Cane'*

FICUS ELASTICA 'DECORA' (fī'–kus ē–las'–ti–kà dē–kôr'–à) comes from Indonesia. You will know it by its common name, 'Rubber Plant.' The leaves are ponderously heavy and large, deep glossy green with prominent veins. The ivory midrib is red beneath and the sheaf of the emerging tips is red. It is a plant which deservingly demands to be noticed. It wants a night temperature of 62 to 65 degrees and needs to be kept moist. Commercial growers plant two or three in a pot and the effect is extremely pleasing.

HOYA CARNOSA (hoi'–a kär–nō'–sa) comes from Queensland and South China and is called 'Wax Plant' because of the waxy, wheel-shaped, pinkish white flowers with red, star-shaped crown. The flowers are fragrant and grow in pendant umbels. This plant takes its time to bloom, but when it does it is worth waiting for. It will bloom repeatedly from the same pedicle; do not cut it off if you wish repeated bloom. It wants bright sun, but can adapt itself to much less light. Let it approach dryness between watering except when it is blooming. Then keep it slightly moist for that period. Its preferred nighttime temperature range is large—50 to 65 degrees. *See page 122.*

MONSTERA DELICIOSA (mon'–stēr–a dē–lis–i–ō–sà) comes from South Mexico and Guatemala. This is a large, climbing plant with leaves that can grow to two feet. It produces long, aerial roots. The leaves are thick, leathery and glossy green. They are pinnately cut and perforated with oblong holes. It produces a boat-shaped white spathe. This is another durable plant, well suited for standing alone in formidable beauty. It wants to be kept moist in a night temperature of 62 to 65 degrees. When this plant grows taller than you wish, do not hesitate to cut off the top, newly emerging leaves.

PEPEROMIA (pe–pēr–ō'–mi–a) comes from South America in a large variety. All of them are excellent plants to keep

CISSUS RHOMBIFOLIA, *'Grape Ivy'*

under lamps on small tables. They want a night temperature of 62 to 65 degrees and need to become crumbly
dry between waterings. We keep a few varieties in our
Dutch sink under a 60-watt bulb, and they do a fine job
of beautifying our dining room. *Peperomia caperata*
(ka–pe–rā′–ta) known as 'Emerald Ripple' has short,
branching stems with dense clusters of roundish, heart-
shaped or peltate leaves, deeply corrugated and quilted.
The color is forest green. *Peperomia fosteri* (fos′–te–rī) is
a creeper with thick foliage in whorls along red stems.
The leaves are forest green, small and elliptical. *Peperomia 'Pixie'* is a clustering small plant of miniature
branches and tiny, ovate, succulent leaves that are grass
green. These are small plants, utterly charming.
See pages 124 and 126.

PHILODENDRON (fil–ō–den′–dron) comes from the area Brazil
to Venezuela. This is a plant too much ignored recently.
The very large variety of this species affords all kinds of
decorative foliage from the *Philodendron cordatum*
(kôr–dā′–tum) with its climbing leaves to the *Philodendron
selloum* (sel–lōm′) which has lush, dark green, pendant,
two-foot leaves, all growing from the center of the plant.
If you have a fairly large space in a corner of a room
which seems difficult to adorn, put the selloum there.
You need nothing else to make that corner outstandingly
conspicuous. The leaves flare out with dramatic grace.
All varieties of the philodendron want to be kept evenly
moist, at a night temperature of 62 to 65 degrees. These
plants are not fussy; they thrive with little care.

RHAPSIS EXCELSA (rā′–pis ex–sel′–sa) comes from South China
and is called 'Large Lady Palm.' Its bamboolike canes
can grow to twelve feet or more. It has thin stems densely
matted with coarse fiber, forming clumps for underground suckers. The leathery, glossy green leaves are
divided into three to ten broad segments. It is a durable

DRACAENA MARGINATA, *'Dwarf Dragon Tree'*

plant, needing a night temperature of 50 to 55 degrees and needs to be kept wet.

SANSEVIERIA (san–se–vi–ē′–ri- a) There are many varieties of this exceedingly tough plant which comes from tropical Africa and all of them are excellent for areas of minimal light. Nothing will happen to this plant if you must neglect it for fairly long periods, and it becomes dry and stays dry. All varieties want a night temperature of 62 to 65 degrees and can be kept moist or can remain dry for a week or ten days. *Sanseveriea surculosa* (sur–ku–lō′–sa) is a stocky, symmetrical rosette of erect, oblanceolate, plain, dark green leaves. *Sanseveriea parva* is a dense rosette of narrowly lanceolate, fresh green leaves with dark crossbanding. This plant can be grown in a basket.

SCINDAPSUS AUREUS (sin–dap′–sus â′–rē–us) is called 'Devil's Ivy' and is known commercially as 'Pothos' (pä–thos). It comes from the Solomon Islands. It is a vine with waxy, dark green leaves with yellow variegation. Here also you will find many varieties. All of them will appreciate a night temperature of 62 to 65 degrees. They want to be kept between dry and moist. If allowed to remain dry for a day or two, the Scindapsus waits very patiently and keeps well.

SPATHIPHYLLUM 'CLEVELANDII' (spath–i–fil′–um klēv–land′–i–ī) comes from South America and is a strong house plant. The leaves are large, lanceolate and leathery, deep green with sunken veins. The inflorescence grows on reedlike stems with ovate-pointed, white papery spathe which turns apple green as it grows older. For a long while with only artificial lighting it can make a vivid picture in a hall without a window. It wants a night temperature of 62 to 65 degrees and needs to be kept wet.

SYNGONIUM PODOPHYLLUM (sin–gō′–nē–um pō–dō–fil′–um)

DRACAENA FRAGRANS MASSANGEANA, *'Corn Plant'*

comes from South America. It trails or climbs and its many varieties are easy to grow. Podophyllum is a small plant with arrow-shaped, thin, green leaves on slender petioles. Later on, the leaves become lobed and then palmately divided into five to nine segments. It wants a night temperature of 62 to 65 degrees and needs to be kept moist.

FICUS BENJAMINA 'EXOTICA,' 'Weeping Java Fig'

Other Plants Which Grow
Well in Low Light Intensity

BROMELIADS

The pineapple family of plants include some of the most distinctively excellent house plants. These Bromeliads (brō–mē–lī–ad) come from Central and South America where they grow amicably on trees, the shallow roots clinging to the branches but not depriving the tree of any of its own nourishment or damaging it in any way. They live on food borne by the rain which they store in their vase-shaped centers. They can also grow on the forest floor. Usually their shape is in the form of a rosette of leathery, concave leaves. Some are plain. Some are bizarrely designed or variegated. Their flowers hide deep in the center of the rosette framed by brilliantly colored leaves or grow tall on showy spikes between highly colored bracts or on panicles of bright, long-lasting berries. The pineapple brings forth our delicious tasting fruit.

The rosette of tough leaves provides a vase-shaped center into which water is poured and in which it is stored. The care of these plants is markedly easy, since a glance suffices to inform you of its need for water.

Bromeliads can live and even bloom in an unfavorable light area, in the center of your living room on the coffee

FICUS ELASTICA 'DECORA,' 'India Rubber Plant'

table. Peatmoss is a good potting medium with sand and horticultural charcoal (not cooking briquettes) added. Osmunda fiber is an excellent material to use for potting material, but is sometimes difficult to get. Some of the Bromeliads we have grown and enjoyed are in the following list:

AECHMEA CHANTINII (ēk–mē'–a shan–tē'–ni–ī) is a colorful, open rosette of large, hard, olive green leaves with marked pinkish gray crossbands. The inflorescence (its flower—pronounced in-flo-res-ence) is on a branched spike of light red bracts tipped yellow. It wants a night temperature of 62 to 65 degrees. Keep water in the cup and keep the potting medium moist. This plant has a sculptured quality that lends formal beauty to a room.

AECHMEA FASCIATA (ēk–mē'–a fäsh–ē–ä'–ta) is called 'Silver King.' It has leathery leaves which are almost completely frosted with silver. Occasional bands •of bluish green cross the leaves. The inflorescence has rose-colored, globose heads and blue flowers. The inflorescence blooms for six months or more. It wants a night temperature of 62 to 65 degrees. Keep water in the cup at all times and keep the potting medium moist. This is another variety of the Bromeliads which is a living sculpture.
See page 132.

AECHMEA FOSTERIANA (fos–tēr–ē–än'–à) is a tubular rosette of pale green to reddish green leaves with purplish brown, irregular mottling and green spines. The flower spike has panicles of crimson bracts and rich yellow petals. It wants a night temperature of 62 to 65 degrees. Keep water in the cups and keep the potting medium moist.

AECHMEA X MAGINALII (mä–ji–nä'–lē) is an open rosette with broad, soft, leathery, olive green, glaucous leaves which

HOYA CARNOSA, *'Wax Plant'*

are red purple underneath. The inflorescence has oblong, berry-like salmon-red bracts tipped with deep blue flowers. It wants a night temperature of 62 to 65 degrees and a moist potting medium. Keep water in the cup.

AECHMEA TILLANDSIOIDES (ti–land–soi'–i–dēz) is a small rosette with narrow, leathery, grayish leaves armed with marginal spines. The inflorescence has green, yellowish or red serrated floral bracts. The flower petals are yellow, followed by berries which are white at first and then turn blue. It wants a night temperature of 62 to 65 degrees. Keep water in the cups and keep the potting medium moist.

CRYPTANTHUS BROMELIOIDES "TRICOLOR" (krip–tan'–thus brō–mē–lē–oi'–dēz trī'–ku–lôr) is called 'Rainbow Star.' It is strikingly variegated with fleshy, fresh green leaves edged and striped ivory white. The margins and base are tinted carmine rose. When it is kept in bright light or filtered sunlight, the leaves will turn pink. It wants a night temperature of 62 to 65 degrees; let it become dry between waterings. Do not water more than once a week or ten days during winter, more often during summer if it is outdoors. This is a charming, colorful addition to your collection, especially when the leaves turn pink.

GUZMANIA LINGULATA VAR. MINOR (guz–mā'–ni–à ling–ū–lā'–ta var. mi–nor) is a small, clustering rosette of thin, leathery yellow green leaves with maroon lines. The bracts are bright orange red with small white flowers. It wants a night temperature of 62 to 65 degrees and needs to approach dryness between waterings.

GUZMANIA MUSAICA (guz–mā'–ni–à mūz'–a–kä) is a rosette of broad, pea-green leaves marked with crossbands consisting of multiple wavy lines colored dark green to red brown. Underneath the leaves are purplish with darker

PEPEROMIA OBTUSIFOLIA, *'Pepper-face'*

lines. The flower spike has red-lined bract leaves; the lead has orange red bracts and golden flowers tipped with white. It wants a night temperature of 62 to 65 degrees. Keep water in the center and the potting medium moist.

NEOREGELIA CAROLINAE 'TRICOLOR' (nē–ō–re–jēl–ē–a ka–rō–lē'–nī) has glossy green leaves with lengthwise bands of ivory white. At flowering time, the leaves become carmine red and spread flat and open as if they were inviting you to notice the center, where small violet purple flowers, edged with white, bloom. This plant exhibited on a low table is magnificent as it opens itself to the full inspection of its admirer. It wants a night temperature of 62 to 65 degrees. Keep water in the center and keep the potting medium moist.

TILLANDSIA IONANTHA (ti– land'–zē–à ī–ō–nan'–thà) if fittingly called 'Little Hedgehog.' It is a charming miniature rosette, only two to four inches high. It has numerous, overlapping, recurving leaves, fleshy and channeled, green on the outside and covered with silvery bristles. It has a sessile inflorescence with violet flowers. It is most interesting mounted on bark embedded in a medium of either osmunda fiber or sphagnum moss. It wants a night temperature of 50 to 65 degrees. Keep it on the dry side; do not water more than once a week or ten days in winter. If it is mounted, immerse the whole thing in water.

TILLANDSIA PLUMOSA (ti–land'–zē–a plū–mō'–sa) is also small. It has a rosette six inches high with dense, threadlike, recurving, soft leaves, silvery gray green. The inflorescence is slightly stalked with spreading floral bracts and narrow violet petals. It wants a night temperature of 50 to 65 degrees. Keep it on the dry side. Do not water more than once a week in winter.

Basket of PEPEROMIA GRISEO-ARGENTEA

VRIESEA FOSTERIANA (vrē'–zi–a fos–tēr–i–a'–ná) is a showy rosette of stiff, nile green to bluish leaves marked with irregular, dark green pencil lines. The inflorescence grows tall and has pale yellow flowers with greenish bracts. It wants a night temperature of 50 to 65 degrees. Keep water in the vase center but do not water the potting medium itself; keep the potting medium on the dry side.

VRIESEA X MARIAE (ma–rē'–à) is called 'Painted Feather,' another spectacular plant when in bloom. It has apple green foliage, tinted pink, and a showy, flattened, featherlike spike with bracts salmon rose at the base and yellow dotted with brown toward the apex. The flowers are yellow and appear along the edges of the spike. It wants a night temperature of 50 to 55 degrees. Keep water in the vase center, and keep the potting medium on the dry side.

VRIESEA SPLENDENS (splen–denz') is called the 'Flaming Sword.' It is a leathery rosette of slender, bluish green leaves marked with deep purple crossbands. The flower spike is long and shaped like a sword with flattened, fiery red bracts and yellow flowers. It is a spectacular plant. It wants a night temperature of 50 to 65 degrees. Keep water in the vase center and keep the potting medium on the dry side.

Either concurrently with its blooming or directly after or in some cases like Vriesea x mariae before its blooming period, Bromeliads produce offshoots. Once the plant has bloomed it will die, but it takes a long time to do that. The leaves remain arrestingly beautiful long after the inflorescence has dried and been cut away. Eventually the leaves will turn yellow and die, but the offshoots provide you with new plants which in their turn will bloom just like their parents. You may separate the offshoot from its parent when it is approximately half the size of the adult. The roots are shallow and you may either break off or cut away the offshoot.

CHAMAEROPS HUMILIS, 'European Fanpalm'

Plants Which Need Good Light

FERNS

Ferns are found wild all over the world. They include plants which vary in size from a creeping stem bearing single, moss-like leaves to tall palm-like treeferns. Their leaves are called fronds. Some have creeping rhizomes which give them quaint common names, like rabbit's foot fern.

The ferns selected in the following list are the ones best suited for home growing. None of them needs direct sunshine, but all of them appreciate good light like that coming in an unobstructed northern window.

ADIANTUM DECORUM 'PACIFIC MAID' (ad–i–an'–tum dē–kôr'–um) comes from Peru. It is a compact plant with two to three pinnate fronds. The pinnae are stiffly set in stages above each other. The leaflets are large, satiny green with veins running into the sinus. It wants a night temperature of 62 to 65 degrees and to be kept wet. Keep it in a northern exposure where it will get strong light.

ASPARAGUS PLUMOSUS (as–par–a–gus plū–mō'–sus) comes from South Africa and is called the 'Fern asparagus.' It

129

PHILODENDRON SELLOUM, a *'Self-Heading Philodendron'*

is a climber with lacy, fern-like green fronds of needle-like branchlets arranged on thin, wiry stems with sharp prickles. It wants a night temperature of 50 to 55 degrees and needs to be kept moist.

ASPLENIUM NIDUS (as–plē'–ni–um nī'–dus) comes from India, Japan and Queensland and is called the 'Birdsnest fern.' It is an attractive rosette of oblanceolate leaves spreading stiffly. The fronds are thin, leathery, green with blackish midrib and wavy margin. It wants a 50- to 55-degree night temperature and needs to be kept wet. *See page 138.*

CYRTOMIUM FALCATUM (sēr–tō'–mi–um fal–kā'–tum) is called the 'Holly Fern.' It comes from Japan, China and India. It has pinnate fronds on brown, scaly stalks. The leaflets are ovate, leathery and dark green. They are slender-pointed. This plant wants a 50- to 55-degree night temperature and needs to be kept moist.

DAVALLIA FEJEENSIS (da–val'–i–à fē–jēen'–sis) comes from the Fiji Islands. It is called 'Rabbit's foot fern' because of the brown, woolly, creeping rhizomes from which the fronds grow, graceful fronds with wiry stems. It wants a night temperature from 50 to 65 degrees and needs to be kept moist. This plant makes a beautiful basket.

DAVALLIA GRIFFITHIANA (gri–fith'–ē–a–na) comes from India and South China. It has creeping rhizomes covered with glistening white scales, wiry fronds three to four, pinnatifid into segments with deeply toothed leaflets. It wants to be kept moist and a night temperature ranging from 50 to 65 degrees.

NEPHROLEPIS EXALTATA BOSTONIENSIS COMPACTA (nē–frol'–e–pis eks–âl–tā'–ta bos–tōn–i–en'–sis kum–pak'–ta) is the 'Dwarf Boston Fern.' It has wide, pinnate fronds, green and spreading. It wants a night temperature of 50 to 55 degrees. Keep it moist.

AECHMEA FASCIATA, *'Silver King'*

NEPHROLEPIS EXALTATA 'WHITMANII' (nē–frol'–e–pis eks–âl–tā'–ta wit'–man–i) comes from Florida and South America. It is called 'Fluffy Ruffles.' It is a dwarf variety with stiff, upright fronds, closely drawn together, dark green. It wants a night temperature of 50 to 55 degrees and this fern *prefers filtered sunlight.* Keep it moist.

PELLAEA ROTUNDIFOLIA (pe–lē'–a rō–tun–di–fō'–li–á) comes from New Zealand. It is a small fern with creeping rhizomes and pubescent stems. Fronds stay near the soil, pinnate, evenly spaced leaflets which are round when young. Later, they are oblong, dark green, waxy and leathery. It likes a 50- to 55-degree night temperature and needs to be kept moist.

PLATYCERIUM BIFURCATUM (plat–i–sē'–ri–um bī–fer–kā'–tum) comes from East Australia, New Guinea and is called 'Staghorn Fern.' It grows easily and produces young plants on its roots. The basal fronds are kidney-shaped and lobed, dark green and thinly covered with white, stellate hairs. It tolerates a range of night temperature of 50 to 65 degrees, and needs to be kept moist. *See page 140.*

POLYSTICHUM TSUS–SIMENSE (pō lis'–ti–kum tsus–si–mencé) comes from the island of Tsus–sima in the Straits of Korea. It is a dwarf fern, shapely tufted and it can be used for terrariums. It has leathery, small, lanceolate, dark green fronds, bipinnate in the lower part. The segments gradually grow smaller toward the slender point and are sharply toothed. It can tolerate a very wide range of night temperatures from 45 to 65 degrees. Keep it moist.

PTERIS CRETICA 'WILSONII' (tē'–vis kre'–ti–ka wil–sōn–i–ī) comes from Florida, Italy and Ethiopa. It is called the 'Table Fern.' It grows low and bushy. The fronds are fresh green, and fork toward the tips into broad, dense crests. It wants a night temperature of 50 to 55 degrees and needs to be kept moist.

CRYPTBERGIA X RUBRA, a Bromeliad

Plants for Areas of Bright, Unobstructed Sunlight for at Least Four Hours Daily

ABUTILON (a–bū'–ti–lon) is an American species called 'Flowering Maple,' although actually it is related to the hollyhock. It wants a 50- to 55-degree night temperature, lots of sun because it flowers profusely, and to be kept moist. The different hybrids produce papery, bell-shaped flowers either white, yellow, salmon or red. This is a plant that blooms best when it is pot-bound. The foliage is pubescent, soft green, resembling maple leaves. Like the hibiscus, it blooms from the tips of fresh growth so early, continuous pinching out in its very young stages will make a full, bushy plant before it reaches the period of blooming. For airy grace, the abutilon excels.

CARISSA GRANDIFLORA (kà–ris'–a gran–di–flō'–ra) is called 'Natal Plum' because it comes from Natal. It is a spiny shrub with dark, shiny, ovate leaves and fragrant white, star-shaped flowers. It produces plumlike red fruit. It appreciates an intermediate night temperature of 50 to 55 degrees and it wants to be kept moist. Without flowers or fruit, its curving branches continually captivate the eye.

135

BILLBERGIA NUTANS, 'Queen's Tears,' a Bromeliad

CITRUS LIMON 'MEYER' AND CITRUS MITIS (si'–trus mī'–tis). The Citrus mitis, Calamondin Orange (kal-a-mon-din) from the Philippines is a small tree with upright slender branches and broad oval, leathery leaves on narrowly winged petioles. The fragrance of the small white flowers is delightfully sweet.

The Calamondin produces small, round fruit about one-half inch in diameter, loose-skinned, deep orange-yellow in color. It needs as much sun as possible, a night temperature of 50 to 55 degrees and between waterings, it wants to become not crumbly dry on top but semidry. It is a fragrant, bright ornament in your very sunny window.

These conditions also pertain to the Citrus limon "Meyer," which is a hybrid of lemon and sweet orange. This plant as well as the lime will produce delicious fruit for your table. Citrus limon 'Meyer' comes from China. The lime is an American hybrid. *See page 142.*

CRASSULA ARGENTEA (kras'–ū–la är–jen'–tē–á) is called the 'Jade Plant.' It comes from South Africa. It wants to be cool at night, 50 to 55 degrees, and it thrives in sunshine although it can keep well for a rather long period without it. It wants to become crumbly dry between waterings. Its leaves are fleshy and thick, spatulate. The upper surface of the leaf is rounded, the lower flat. It is a glossy jade green. In direct outdoor summer sun the leaves will turn red, but if you wish to keep them green, put the plant in a filtered sunlight area or a spot in bright light without sun. When they are old, they produce a pinkish, white flower worth waiting for. But even without its bloom, this plant with its sturdy, thick main stem and Oriental tree-like appearance is a most satisfactory foliage plant. *See page 144.*

CUPHEA HYSSOPIFOLIA (kú'–fē–á hi–sup–i–fō'–li–a) is called 'Elfin Herb,' and delights your eye with the tiny, lavender flowers with which the plant intermittently throughout the year is covered. It comes from Mexico and

ASPLENIUM NIDUS, *'Bird's Nest Fern'*

Guatemala. It is a small, woody shrub that will love your sunny window and there is no doubt that you will come to love it. Its leaves are tiny and linear. Keep it in direct sunshine for as long as possible daily. It wants to be kept moist and its preferred nighttime temperature is 50 to 55 degrees.

EUPHORBIA MILII VAR. SPLENDENS (ū–fôr′–bi–á mi′–li–ī) comes from Madagascar and is called 'Crown of Thorns.' It wants a night temperature from 50 to 65 degrees, as much sun as possible, and it needs to become crumbly dry between waterings. If you keep it moist, the branches become mushy, rot and die. In its native habitat, it thrives with very little moisture. It has scandent stems with spines. The leaves are dull green and the flower bracts are salmon red with a pale center.

X FATSHEDERA LIZEI (x–fats–hed′–e–rä li′–ze–ī) is a hybrid from Japan and French parents. If you have a sunny area where you want a tall plant, Fatshedera answers most suitably although it can also live in a sunless area. It grows rapidly, would like a low nighttime temperature of anywhere from 40 to 55 degrees, and it wants to be kept moist always. Because it grows tall rapidly, it will need support. In order to force it to branch, cut out the top growth frequently when the plant is young. It has five-lobed, leathery leaves which are shining, dark green.

FELICIA AMELLOIDES (fe–lis′–i–à a–mel–oi′–dēz) comes from South Africa and is called 'Blue Daisy.' It wants a night temperature of 50 to 55 degrees, lots of sun and it wants to be kept moist. It is a shrubby plant with opposite, obovate leaves and daisy-like flowers with sky-blue florets and yellow disks on long stalks. It will bloom all winter.

GREVILLEA ROBUSTA (gre–vil′–ē–a rō–bus′–ta) is another plant which grows tall rapidly. It comes from New South Wales and is called 'Silk Oak,' an appropriate name for the dainty, lacy foliage. It appreciates direct sunlight, wants

PLATYCERIUM WILHELMINAE-REGINAE, *'Staghorn Fern'*

to be watered whenever the top soil is slightly dry, and it likes a night temperature of 50 to 55 degrees. Its shoots are silvery, the leaves are green and fern-like, silky-haired and bipinnate into finely lobed segments. When young, pinch out frequently to insure side growth.

GYNURA PROCUMBENS (jī–nū'–ra prō–kum'–benz) is called the 'Velvet Plant.' It hails from Java. It likes a warm night temperature of 62 to 65 degrees, appreciates lots of sun and wants to be kept moist. The deep purple of its leaves makes it a striking plant. The leaves are fleshy, covered with violet or purple hairs and the orange flowers produce a stark contrast with the leaves. The hot summer sun will bleach the purple color, so protect it.

HEDERA HELIX 'SHAMROCK' (hed'–ēr–a hē'–lix) comes from the Azores and Canaries. It needs bright sunshine and wants to be kept moist. Its red stems have tiny, bright green, three-lobed leaves with small intervals between the nodes. It wants bright sunshine, likes to be moist and will take a night temperature of 40 to 55 degrees.

HIBISCUS ROSA–SINENSIS 'SCARLET' (hī–bis'–kus rō'–za sī–nen'–sis) comes from Australia. It rewards you for your care by producing brilliant scarlet, medium-large flowers regularly throughout the year. It wants as much sun as possible, and it must be kept moist. Its preferred night temperature is 62 to 65 degrees. The leaves are glossy green. Since blooming is only on new shoots, pinching out frequently before the plant is ready to bloom—when it is young—insures a bushy growth. When the plant is older, pruning to insure side and bottom growth will necessarily sacrifice bloom.

HOYA CARNOSA (hoi'–a kär–nō'–sa) is called the 'Wax Plant.' It comes from Queensland and South China; the waxy flowers give it its common name. It accommodates itself to a wide range of night temperatures—50 to 65 degrees—and it needs to become really dry between waterings. Keep it in bright sunshine and patiently await its bloom-

CITRUS MITIS, 'Calamondin Orange'

ing, which is a delight when it occurs, with its wheel-shaped, fragrant, pinkish white flowers, red, star-shaped crown growing in pendant umbels. It is a vine and can be trained upward. Its leaves are elliptic and green. Hoya carnosa variegata has fresh green to bluish leaves with a creamy white or pink border. *See page 122.*

MALPIGHIA COCCIGERA (mal–pig'–i–a cōk–i–jē'–ra) is called the 'Miniature Holly.' It comes from the West Indies. Keep it in the sun; allow it to become dry between waterings. When it blooms, do not let it become quite so dry between waterings. Give it a night temperature of 50 to 55 degrees. It is a bushy, evergreen shrub covered with tiny, hollylike, stiff leaves which are glossy-green. The leaves have coarse, spiny teeth. The plant bears small pink flowers from spring through most of the summer. *See page 146.*

MYRTUS COMMUNIS (mẽr'–tus kom–mūn'–is) is called 'Greek Myrtle.' It is an evergreen, loosely leafed shrub. Keep it in the sun, let it become slightly dry between waterings and give it a night temperature anywhere between 40 and 55 degrees. Its leaves are dark green, broad-ovate and about two inches long; they give off a spicy scent when rubbed or bruised. Older plants will produce fragrant white flowers with numerous stamens and purple black berries.

NICODEMIA DIVERSIFOLIA (ni–kō–dēm'–i–à dī–vẽr–si–fō'–li–a) is called 'Indoor Oak' because its leaves are shaped like those of an English oak. Give it sunshine, keep it moist, and give it a night temperature of 62 to 65 degrees. It is a woody plant with thin, leathery, quilted leaves. The margins of the leaves are lobed and undulate. The surface has a metallic blue sheen. The petioles are bronze. It comes from Madagascar.

OSMANTHUS FRAGRANS (oz–man'–thus frā'–granz) is one of the loveliest of all house plants. It is called 'Sweet Olive' and it will flower intermittently throughout the year,

CRASSULA ARGENTEA, *'Jade Plant'*

perfuming an entire room with the fragrance of its tiny white flowers. Give it as much sunshine as possible, keep it moist, and give it a night temperature anywhere between 40 and 55 degrees. We have a 'Sweet Olive' which is about five feet tall in our plant room, and it has adapted itself extremely well to the higher night temperature. It comes from the Himalayas, China and South Japan. It has wiry twigs and holly-shaped, stiff, olive green leaves, finely toothed at the margins. As soon as we enter our plant room, the 'Sweet Olive' welcomes us above all other scents with its subtle, delicate sweetness.

PITTOSPORUM TOBIRA (pi–tos'–pō–rum tō–bī'–ra) comes from China and Japan and is an extremely fine house shrub. It wants to become crumbly dry between waterings and it likes the sun—as much as it can get. Its night temperature is 40 to 55 degrees. It is a tough, shapely evergreen. The leaves are thick and leathery, obovate in shape, dark, shining green. It bears terminal clusters of small, creamy-white flowers.

PODOCARPUS MACROPHYLLA (pod–ō–kär'–pus mak–rō–fi'–la) comes from China and Japan and is called 'Buddhist Pine.' It wants a nighttime temperature between 40 and 55 degrees. It thrives beautifully either in direct sun, in filtered sunlight or in lesser light. It is a dioecious, coniferous shrub with horizontal branches, crowded leafy twigs, leathery, deep green, narrow, linear-lanceolate, needle-like leaves. White fragrant axillary flowers appear followed by bluish purple berries. *See page 148.*

PUNICA GRANATUM 'NANA' (pū'–ni–ka gra–nā'–tum na–na) ranges from Iran to the Himalayas. It is called 'Dwarf Pomegranate' and it will bloom intermittently throughout the year. Give it all the sunlight possible, keep it moist, and give it a 50- to 55-degree night temperature. Not only is this plant one of the most appealing with its

MALPIGHIA COCCIGERA, *'Miniature Holly'*

orange red flowers, crumpled petals and purple calyx, it creates a feeling of timelessness, of ancient wonder—the pomegranate of the Bible. It produces edible fruit, orange outside and deep-yellow to red inside. The leaves are shining, oblong, three-quarters of an inch to three inches long.

ROSMARINUS OFFICINALIS (ros–ma–rī'–nus o–fi–shi–nā'–lis) is the herb rosemary which you use in cooking. It is called the 'Dew of the Sea' and comes from the Mediterranean. Smell it for a most savory pleasure. It wants bright sunshine, a chance to become really dry between waterings, and a night temperature of 50 to 55 degrees. It has needle-like leaves which are grayish, shiny above and white downy beneath. It produces light blue flowers in spikes from the tip of the branches. *See page 150.*

BRASSAIA ACTINOPHYLLA (bra'–si–à ak–tin–ō–fi'–la) is commonly called Schefflera (shef'-le-ra), comes from Java, New Guinea. It is known as the 'Australian Umbrella Tree.' It wants to become crumbly dry between waterings. It likes bright sunshine or good light and a 62- to 65-degree night temperature. The leaves grow in umbrella-like clusters. If you are impatient for a large tub plant, Schefflera will accommodate you quickly.
See page 152.

TRIPOGANDRA MULTIFLORA (tri–pō–gan'–dra mul–ti–flō–ra) comes from Jamaica. It branches freely with slender stems and small, narrow, ovate, olive green leaves which are purplish beneath. It bears clusters of small, white flowers. In a basket it quickly grows into a round, ball-like pattern, and it is a most cheerful sight with its myriads of white flowers. It wants bright sunshine. Keep it moist and give it a night temperature of 62 to 65 degrees.

PODOCARPUS MACROPHYLLA MAKI, *'Southern Yew'*

XI

Pests and Troubles

There is no better protection against pests and other troubles than to buy your plants from a reputable greenhouse where they have been protected by a routine, rigorous program of chemical spraying to guarantee their well-being and their freedom from disease. The second safety measure is to use a sterilized potting mix, which is what you will be purchasing when you buy the commercially packaged product. The third measure of protection for your plants is to wash them thoroughly once a month. We cannot stress enough the importance of this hygiene.

However, you should become familiar with certain insects so that you will be able to recognize and get rid of them quickly. Fortunately, the variety of insects which commonly attack plants is not large so it is easy to become familiar enough to be able to recognize them and their effect upon plants.

If you wonder where these insects come from the answer is from anywhere. They are clothes-borne by a visitor to your home or greenhouse; they are airborne and come through an opening door or even through the fine mesh of the window screen, since they are so tiny.

The list of sucking insects includes aphids, mealy bugs, white fly and scale.

149

ROSMARINUS OFFICINALIS, *'Rosemary'*

APHIDS

Description: Aphids are plant lice and cluster on both sides of the leaf. They particularly enjoy the tender tips of new growth and emerging flower buds. They can be green, brown, gray or red. They are tiny and soft-bodied. They secrete a sticky, colorless excrement on the leaves and stems. If this excrement, which is called "honey dew" is not washed off, it attracts a black fungus which is noticeable and most unattractive. The first time you notice this phenomenon is the first time you utter the words "honey dew" in a markedly ironic voice.

Effect Upon Plant: Aphids puncture the leaf and stem with their proboscises and suck the plant juice. When you see aphids, do not rush for the chemical spray can. Aphids can be easily washed off. The trick, however, is to keep washing. Aphids are remarkably prolific and in two days' time you can have a host of new aphids who immediately become busy at sucking plant juices and creating another new generation. Therefore, wash at intervals of two—or at the most three—days until you are certain that you have rid yourself of all eggs. Look particularly at the undersides of the leaves and new tips and buds.

MEALY BUGS

Description: Mealy bugs are white, soft-bodied insects covered with a powdery, waxy substance which gives them the appearance of masses of cotton. They cluster in the crotch of the stem and appear also on the underside of the leaves. Wash them off with warm water. Use a Q-tip if you find it difficult to remove the entire cottony mass from the crotches of the stem. Mealy bugs live by sucking sap.

Effect Upon Plant: Mealy bugs cause sickly foliage and bud drop on flowering plants. If not removed, they will

BRASSAIA ACTINOPHYLLA, 'Schefflera'
'Australian Umbrella Tree'

kill the plant. Once they appear, inspect the plant every three days for reappearance of the bug.

RED SPIDERS

Description: Red spiders are so tiny that it is difficult to see them without a hand lens. Red spiders thrive where the air is hot and dry. They live on the underside of the leaves and spin webs.

Effect on Plants: Red spiders suck the plant sap; the effect is a spotty, rust-colored speckling of the leaves until they finally dry up and fall off. Washing at intervals of three days will be effective. Whenever you see a web on your plants, it will be safer to wash them even though the web may have been spun by a harmless house spider. It is difficult to distinguish between the web of a harmless spider and the web of the tiny, destructive red spider. So wash away.

SCALE

Description: Scale is a small, sucking insect which in its adult stage is stationary. Scale may be colored tan, brown, black or white. Its shape is oval, oblong or circular. The adult scale is protected by a shell in which the eggs are laid. The young move to new locations when they hatch and develop scales of their own into which the female lays the eggs of the next generation. The shell protects them from insecticides. Therefore they must be dislodged. You can use your fingernail to dislodge the shells. Then wash the plant. Observe the plant at intervals and watch for the formation of new shells. Washing will remove the young before they form the shells.

Effect Upon Plant: Like all sucking insects, they drain the vitality and vigor from the plant.

SLUGS

Description: Slugs are easily seen if they are present—
clinging to the side of the pot or curled up in the drainage holes or upon the leaves. Usually they hide during
the day and emerge at night to chew the leaves. Sometimes they chew during the day as well. Slugs are snails
without shells.

Effect Upon Plant: Slugs chew holes in leaves that are so
perfectly round you might think a mechanical drill had
been at work. If you see such a hole, look for a slug. You
can also detect slugs by the slimy trail they leave. They
rob the plant of its vigor. Pick the slug off and destroy it.
Do not just drop it into the wastepaper basket. They
look lethargic, but they can move at a surprisingly rapid
pace up the basket and out on the floor to climb again
into a plant victim.

You will observe that we advocate washing plants with a
mildly forceful flow of warm water for all of the above sucking
insects. We prefer this technique rather than the technique of
chemical control particularly if there are small children in the
household. However, there is one sucking insect that cannot
be washed off. For this, we must advise chemical spraying.
This insect is a fly.

WHITE FLY

Description: It is tiny and it is white and called, therefore, white fly. The adults are mothlike and covered with
a white, waxy powder.

Effect Upon Plant: White flies suck juices from the underside of the leaves. They also secrete the sticky substance
called "honey dew," upon which a sooty fungus fastens.
The reason we must suggest chemical spraying is because
as soon as you touch an infested plant the white fly will

fly away. But it will return to the same plant as soon as you leave it alone. It doesn't wait around to be washed off. For white fly as well as for any of the previously described insects, if you decide to spray at any time, buy a commercial spray which includes Malathion and Kelthane. Follow the instructions on the can carefully and observe the proper distance you must stand from the plant because the emerging spray will freeze plant leaves if the can is held too close to them. In winter, isolate the plant in a room which will not be used for the rest of the day and then spray. In summer, you can spray outdoors. In this ecological age, the spraying we do should be a last-resort technique. Carefully observe the directions for the quantity of chemical per plant sprayed. Remember also that it is the *underside* of the leaf which primarily should be sprayed because that is where the young gather.

A novel method of attempting to liquidate white fly is to prepare the vacuum cleaner for use near the infested plant. Turn it on. Now shake the plant slightly. The white fly will immediately fly up and you can suck it up with the vacuum hose. That will take care of the adult fly. Wash the young from the undersides of the leaves. They are stationary, and can be easily removed.

XII

Propagation

The Chinese, according to a story long remembered, are so gracious that they insist on bestowing any object admired by a guest. This trait becomes the lovely quality of every budding horticulturist. No guest in your home will admire your plants without stirring in you an ardent desire, if not to give them, at least to share them. Therefore, not only does a knowledge of propagation become a financial essential, it allows your unselfish generosity to blossom without making inroads into your own cherished collection.

There are many propagation techniques. Some of them we shall describe in detail. Some we shall only name, so you will know there are other methods to pursue as you become more experienced and skilled.

We trace the origin of our cultivated plants to three developments: first, some plants were selected by man for cultivation from wild species and evolved into radically different forms; second, other plants evolved as hybrids between species and have no single wild relative; third, other groups of plants occurred naturally. Most cultivated plants will either be lost or will revert to less desirable forms unless they are propagated under controlled conditions that preserve their unique characteristics.

The two categories of propagation which include all

methods are sexual propagation and vegetative propagation.

Sexual propagation is seed propagation. Seed is the result of a sexual process which involves the union of sperm and egg cells—sperm from the stamen of the flower and egg cells from the pistil. Some plants are sterile and cannot produce seed. This is especially true of certain hybrids. Vegetative propagation is the only way to reproduce these plants. Other hybrids set seeds. However, in seed or sexual propagation, you must expect a certain amount of variation in the seedlings resulting in the possibility of a new plant with different characteristics.

With vegetative propagation it is possible to duplicate exactly, and virtually to eliminate the possibility of genetic variation. Vegetative propagation includes propagation by runners, suckers, bulblets, leaf and leaf bud cuttings, stem cuttings, root cuttings, division or separation and air- and ground-layering. The theory in vegetative propagation is that each of the millions of tiny living cells which make up every plant has the power to regenerate into the whole plant. Thus, a single leaf, a wedge of leaf, or a stem with leaves growing roots in a favorable medium will eventually produce a whole plant. Therefore, to perpetuate the desirable hybrid characteristics of the parent plants, it is necessary to rely on vegetative propagation.

We shall describe fully how to propagate with seeds and also how to propagate by division or separation, suckers or offshoots, offsets, leaf cuttings, leaf-petiole cuttings, stem cuttings, root cuttings, air-layering and spore propagation. Let these techniques become familiar and easy for you with frequent practice. Other techniques are not difficult by any means. We do not deal with them in this chapter because you are less likely to use them while you are a beginner.

The first techniques we shall deal with are those which need no special rooting material, trays, tray coverings. These methods allow you to place the new plant directly into your sterile potting soil in a small pot because they will already have roots, as we shall soon see.

The easiest and simplest method of propagation is separation or division. When all the stems of a plant emerge from the base, it can be divided into one or more plants. You may do this when the plant has become too large or simply when you want one or two plants to share with friends. Some plants in this category are African violets, Cyperus diffuses, Begonias, Ferns, Sansevieria, Cuphea, Acorus.

The technique is as follows: take a sharp knife, which you have sterilized in alcohol, and slice the plant in half, right through the root. If the halves are large enough, you can slice these in half again, and you will have four plants. Be certain when you slice down that each section of plant will have its equal share of root mass. This technique does not endanger the plant at all. The next step is to cut back the top structure to encourage the plant to produce new shoots. The third step is to pot your new plants directly into sterile potting soil. Easy, isn't it? And it is an excellent way to keep your plants the size you want them to be and also to share them. When plants are low-growing, like the African violet or the Acorus it is not necessary to cut back. This is also true of the Sanseveria and others like it that have leaves that you do not cut back.

Some plants produce suckers or offshoots from the base. Plants in this category are the Bromeliads, Pandanus veitchii. When the offshoots are large enough to handle, break them off from the mother plant or cut them off, making certain that you are cutting a small part of the root with the sucker. We think it is better to wait until the offshoots in the Bromeliad family are half the size of the mother plant before separating them. Sometimes we found it necessary to knock the plant out of its pot in order to cut a sucker away because it is difficult to get hold of it with the roots when the plant is in the pot. Pot the offshoot in sterile potting soil in a small pot, where it will independently develop a large root structure.

Some plants produce offsets which are small plantlets or runners. One example is the plant commonly known as the spider plant (Chlorophytum capense), which sends out plantlets at the end of long runners. These small plantlets can be cut from the mother plant and potted directly into sterile potting medium in small pots, where they will develop more roots.

The techniques that now follow involve a process where the plant material you are using for propagation has no root at all and must develop a root structure in special circumstances. For this type of technique which includes leaf cuttings, leaf-petiole cuttings, stem cuttings, root cuttings and spore propagation, have in readiness the following:

1. Rooting medium, which may be fine sand, perlite or vermiculite. These materials retain moisture and allow good aeration.
2. A clear plastic container of any shape not less than six inches deep, with a lid or cover and several holes punched in the bottom for drainage.
3. A sharp knife which has been sterilized in alcohol.
4. A synthetic plant hormone like Rootone, to prevent rot and to promote rooting.

Fill the plastic container with one of the rooting mediums to about two-thirds of its depth. Moisten the medium thoroughly.

Plants with fleshy leaves or thick petioles can be propagated by leaf cuttings. This category includes most gesneriads, Peperomias, Tolmiea (picky-back plant), African violets, Begonias, succulents. Tropical plants possessing fleshy veins can be propagated by leaf cuttings.

LEAF CUTTINGS: With your sharp, sterile knife, sever a leaf from its petiole (stem), leaving a tiny section of the petiole attached to the leaf. Select a healthy, firm leaf which is not yet full-grown. Turn the leaf over. The veins are more distinct on the back of the leaf. With the tip of your sharp knife, make lengthwise cuts through three main veins about one inch long, and extend the cuts into the tiny section of the petiole.

Dust these cut edges with Rootone. Then, cupping the leaf slightly, insert it into the rooting medium in a diagonal position to about one inch in depth—in fact, to the top of the cut veins. This diagonal position allows light to reach the entire surface of the leaf which is not under the rooting medium. Pack the rooting medium gently and firmly about the leaf, making sure that no part of the cut veins is exposed. Write the name of the plant and the date of its insertion on a plant marker and insert the marker near the cutting. Do not rely on your memory or on your ability to recognize the leaf cutting; it changes its color and appearance as it develops roots, and chances are most certain that you will not recognize it.

Cover the plastic container with its lid, or if it has no lid, with polyethylene material like Saran Wrap, which permits light to enter and keeps the humidity within. Place the container in a good light but out of direct sun. If there is too much moisture condensing on the lid or the polyethylene, uncover the container for a short while—one-half hour to an hour—and then replace. The rooting medium must be kept moist, but not wet. If you have to add moisture, sprinkle it in. You may use the sprinkler which you use to prepare your clothes for ironing.

The rooting time varies from plant to plant—from ten days to two months or more. At the end of a month (or less, if you have reason to believe that roots have formed), scoop up your plant by burrowing your forefinger, middle finger and thumb deeply under the cutting. Lift it out and examine it for roots. If you attempt to pull at the cutting, you may pull it loose from its new and very tender roots. If the roots are at least one inch long, the cutting may be potted in a two and one-quarter-inch or at most two and one-half-inch clay pot. It is not necessary to put crock into this size pot.

When you pot it, place the cutting close to the side of the pot instead of in the center. It will receive more oxygen in that location. If the roots are not long enough, put the cutting back into the propagating medium as you did in the beginning. The propagating medium will cling to the emerging roots. Nevertheless, you will be able to determine whether the roots are long enough. When you pot the cutting, do not attempt to remove the propagating medium.

When you pot, press the cutting into the potting mixture very gently but firmly. At this time, water by placing the pot into a container of water, leaving it there until the top soil of the pot is moistened. Watering from the top at this time may dislodge the cutting from its newly planted position. Keep the cutting in good light for the first few days, but not in sunlight. Do not let it dry out. Keep on watering from the bottom for about two weeks to prevent overwatering. Do not fertilize it for a few weeks. The cutting should remain in its small pot for several months until it satisfies the requirements for transfering to the next-size pot described in the chapter on repotting.

Rex Begonias, which produce large-sized leaves, can be propagated by using a section of the leaf. Cut the leaf into wedge-shaped sections, each one containing at least two main veins. It is not necessary in this instance to slit the veins. Treat these wedge-shaped sections exactly as you would a whole leaf.

You may also use a leaf-petiole cutting. Take a leaf with two inches of stem. After dusting the end of the stem with Rootone, insert it to about one inch in depth into the rooting material. Its position in the rooting material should be diagonal. Press the rooting material firmly about the stem. If the leaf is large, trim the entire leaf to accommodate its size to the plastic container. All you need for propagation is the heart of the leaf where the veins come together into the petiole and about one inch of surrounding leaf. With this type of cutting it is best to let it remain in the rooting medium until small leaves form at the base of the stem.

STEM CUTTINGS: A plant that has stems of branches growing from its base can be propagated by choosing about three to five inches of a sturdy, green (not woody) stem with at least three leaf nodes. Leaf nodes are the places from which a leaf emerges. The best stem cutting is from new growth. Remove all leaves except the three top leaves. If the leaves are large, trim them. All you need is the heart as we explained above. Cut the stem sharply and cleanly right below the third node. Dip the end of the stem into Rootone and insert it into the rooting medium. Its direction in the rooting will be vertical. The remaining procedure is exactly like that for leaf cuttings.

Cane Begonias can be propagated by this method as well as the Abutilon, Carissa grandiflora, Citrus plants, Euphorbia splendens, Gynura sarmentosa, the hibiscus and the Osmanthus.

Some plants produce rhizomes which are underground stems bearing roots and prominent eyes or leafbuds, which can be cut into sections. Many ferns produce these rhizomes. Tubers are modified underground stems set with buds which can be divided into as many pieces as they have eyes.

Ferns form spores on the undersides of their fertile fronds. Propagation of these ferns is as follows:

Cut the spore-bearing frond into one-half-inch pieces and lay them, spore side down, on the surface of the prepared propagating medium. The spores will drift out and sow themselves. When the spores have been discharged, remove the fronds.

Or, gather fronds bearing ripe spore cases, place them in a paper bag and keep the bag in a warm, dry place. In a few days the dustlike spores will be shed and they can be scattered thinly on the surface of the medium.

After the spores are sown, cover the seed pan with a pane of glass and stand it in a container constantly filled with water. Until leaves are visible, never attempt overhead watering.

A flat plate of green tissue will form. It is called the prothalium. With a drop of condensation, male and female organs will mate and develop the true plant. When the prothalium forms, the glass covering should be removed.

It is possible to propagate many cuttings in water, but others will rot. Moreover, the root structure developed in water is not as vigorous as that developed in the suggested rooting mediums. Again, it is possible that a cutting which has developed a fairly good root structure in water will not take kindly to soil when it is potted. If you want to try rooting in water, do so. But if the plant is rare, or hard to come by, we would suggest that you take no chances and that you use sand, vermiculite or perlite instead.

Both seed and vegetative propagation are helped when bottom heat is supplied. But successful propagation has been accomplished without it. However, if you are so inclined, low-voltage heating pads are sold for this purpose.

SEED PROPAGATION: The first requirement is that you buy seeds from an established dealer. If the seeds fail to germinate because they are old, you will not know and you may be disheartened by failure. Therefore, buy good seeds. The container may be borrowed from your kitchen if you can spare a fairly shallow one, approximately two inches deep, into whose bottom you will punch holes at intervals for drainage. Milled sphagnum moss is the best material for the propagation of seeds. It is sterile and will prevent damping off, the fungus disease which is responsible for the death of seedlings. The sphagnum moss holds water well, and you will become familiar quickly with its appearance when it is dry. This is a condition which must not be allowed to occur so becoming familiar with the dry appearance of the moss is essential.

Milled sphagnum moss can be obtained in a garden supply store. The moss is fine and airy, and the best way to moisten it thoroughly is to put it into a pot filled with hot water. See that the sphagnum moss remains submerged until it is wet. When the water is cool enough, take handfuls of the moss and squeeze the water out of it completely. Then line your container with it. Tamp the moss down in the container so that it is flat and level and up to about one-half inch below the rim of the container. It is not necessary to tamp it down hard; do it gently and firmly. Then scatter the seeds thinly over the surface. If the seeds are tiny, put them into a clean salt shaker and shake over the propagating medium. Do not cover them with more milled sphagnum moss. In many species covering inhibits germination. But if the seeds are large, they should be covered with moss to the depth of their own thickness. In this case, take some of the moss between your fingers and shred it over the seeds.

Now water again by submerging your container in another one filled with tepid water. When water appears on top, remove the seed container. The water draining from it will settle the seeds more firmly on the bed of milled sphagnum moss. Keep the moss moist. One drying-out episode can be fatal to the seeds. Bottom watering is definitely preferred in this process.

Cover the container with polyethylene. Ventilate the container daily by lifting the cover for a short while—about ten or fifteen minutes. Keep the container in good light, but not in direct sunshine.

Seeds will germinate in three weeks or three months. If they are tropical plants and do not appear in four months, try again.

As soon as the seedlings sprout their second pair of leaves, you may thin them out by pulling out the seedlings you do not want and discarding them. Naturally, choose those seedlings for discard which are the weakest. When the remaining seedlings have shown some root growth—remember, you dig under them and lift them out for inspection—they can be transplanted into very small clay pots. Make small greenhouses for them by covering them with polyethylene until they seem vigorous enough to go out into the world unaided.

General cautions and reminders are these:

1. Do not let the rooting material dry out.
2. Water from the bottom to prevent overwatering or the dislodgment of the seeds.
3. Ventilate daily.

When you have a large plant which has a fleshy main stem which is no longer pleasing in appearance because it has lost so many bottom leaves, air-layering is the propagating method that will not injure the plant and will result eventually in a new plant. The time this process takes is longer, perhaps a few months. But it is worthwhile. The technique is as follows:

About twelve to fifteen inches below the firm and healthy bottom leaves, make a slanting cut one-third of the way through the stem, cutting upward so fluid will run out. Insert a wooden match minus its sulfur tip into the cut to hold it open. Dust the cut with Rootone. Thoroughly wet a ball of long-fiber sphagnum moss and place it around the cut. The ball of sphagnum should be large enough to anticipate the growth of a good-sized bunch of roots. Try to visualize from the size of the top leaves of your plant the size of the roots that will grow into the sphagnum. Also, realize that this large plant does not produce fine roots; it produces thick roots.

Tightly wind aluminum foil or plastic around the ball of sphagnum and the stem, tying the top and bottom of the foil with black electrical tape.

As soon as roots are well formed (untie the aluminum foil and look), sever the plant below the root-bearing ball of sphagnum. Remove the aluminum foil or plastic, but leave the sphagnum which adheres to the roots. Pot the plant in a pot size suitable to the present size of the plant.

Maintain a high humidity, using already-discussed techniques, around the newly potted plant until the roots have emerged from the sphagnum ball and are firmly established in the soil.

Springtime is the time when there is a resurgence of activity in Nature and new life is not easily denied. It is this time when plants spurt into new growth, and this is the best part of the plant to take for propagation. At The Potting Shed we propagated plants at any season, but we did it under controlled conditions. For the beginner, we suggest that you begin your propagation efforts in the spring of the year so that the gentle benignity of that season will smile upon your efforts and crown them successfully with new plants.

XIII

Names and Identification

We have always wanted to know how things began; in fact, when we were very young, we continualy asked how beginnings began. Naturally, our interest in plants included curiosity about the way in which they began to be named and identified and we think you may share that curiosity. Who named plants? Why were they given certain names? What do their names mean?

In every science and every art, systems of naming are essential in order that the names become significant and understandable to everyone all over the world. Latin is the language which is universally understood by scientists, and therefore Latin names and terms are used.

A system of naming plants has gradually evolved through the efforts of botanists and horticulturists that provides the basis for uniform worldwide plant identification. This system is embodied in the International Code of Botanical Nomenclature for Cultivated Plants. The term *plant nomenclature* means naming plants. The root of the word *nomen* comes from the Latin meaning name.

Our system of plant nomenclature begins with Linnaeus, who is called the Father of Botany. There were many before Linnaeus who named plants, but Linnaeus was the first who

166

founded a system. He was the originator of the binomial method of designating plants and animals. Under the binomial system, every plant has at least two names: the first is the name of the genus or family; the second usually describes the first and is the name of the species. If the plant has a third name, this refers to the variety. By this system of binomial nomenclature, all plants are known by people in all countries who speak or write of them with precision.

Linnaeus was a Swedish botanist, who was born in 1707 and died in 1778. His name originally was Karl von Linne. His first use of specific names was made in his work *Genera Plantarum* published in 1737. It was more fully developed in *Species Plantarum* published in 1753. The 1758 edition of his *Systema Natural* is used by biologists as the basis of Linnaean nomenclature.

The names of some plant species frequently refer to the man or woman who discovered or described the plant. When the species name honors someone, it is usually but not always a botanist. When you see a species name ending in *ii* it is a Latin masculine ending attached to a man's name. The Latin *ae* is a feminine ending attached to a woman's name. Some species names refer to the place where they were first found or a region which they are believed to represent. Names like Americanus, Japonicus, Virginianus, Philadelphicus are self-explanatory.

A great many species names describe the plant, the shape of it or its habit of growing, the color of its leaves or flowers, the fact that you may eat it or that it may poison you, the fact that it is useful as a medicine or that it can be used as a dye.

The complete scientific name of any plant includes: genus, in Latin; species in Latin, and cultivar in the words of a common language. Cultivar names start with a capital initial letter and are set off by single quotation marks. A cultivar is a contraction of the phrase *cultivated variety*. The term *variety* is used synonymously with cultivar.

If the name of a plant is uncertain or if it has only temporary standing, that name is shown in double quotation marks and/or is followed by the abbreviation "hort."

We have been using words like genus, species, cultivar. Cultivar has already been defined. Let us define the first two and add a few additional words for identification:

A *genus* is a subdivision of a family made up of a few or many members (the Latin word for more than one genus is *genera*), which are alike in general characteristics and show a close relationship. A genus contains groups of species.

A *species* is a subdivision of a genus distinct from other kinds in essential features whose members are so closely alike that they may all have come from a single parent. They have obvious structural characterics in common.

A *variety* includes the individuals within a species whose differences are too slight to make up another species.

A *clone* is a variety of plant derived from a single individual by various types of asexual or vegetative propagation.
A *corm* is an enlarged, fleshy, bulblike base of a stem.

When you see the name of a plant which is preceded by the X mark, it designates the generic name of two generic hybrids or Latinized specific names of hybrids derived from two species. This system complies with the rules of the International Code of Nomenclature.

At the very top of this entire system of classification is the larger family name. A family is a major subdivision of an order in the classification of plants usually consisting of several genera and showing close relationship. For instance, the family name for the Begonia is Begoniaceae. It includes only one genus—the Begonia—probably because that genus is an extremely diversified family of at least 1,200 different species.

The pineapple family is called Bromeliaceae and includes

the genera Aechmea, Billbergia, Cryptanthus, Guzmania, and many others.

The family name of the chrysanthemum is Compositae and includes Zinnia, Cineraria, Aster, succulent forms and many others.

The plant you know as the jade plant (Crassula argentea) belongs to the family of Crassulaceae, along with Echeveria, Kalanchoe and Sedum.

It isn't essential to know any part of the above to enjoy plants. But it is always nice to know, isn't it?

XIV

Sources for Plants

If you enjoy every stage of growth, you are the beginner who will relish propagating and who will rejoice at the first tiny set of leaves sprouting from a seed. But if you are less patient, you are the beginner who would rather see a more finished product and who would rather buy a more mature plant.

We consider a plant in a three-inch pot well established. It has passed through at least two years of growth and will indicate whether it is a weakling or one of Nature's fittest.

There are local greenhouses from which to buy, and by this time you know how to look for the essential things in a plant before buying. If you are buying a specimen plant, large and imposing enough to grace by itself an area in your home, you want to buy from a local greenhouse so you can see what you are getting. Even florists are catering to the growing demand for house plants and are increasing their stock of large plants.

However, as you develop experience and a need for varieties which are difficult or impossible to find locally, you will want to order from mail-order houses. Later on in this chapter we shall name and recommend three houses on which you may rely for excellent quality.

Catalogues of greenhouses which ship plants by mail will

specify their shipping seasons. For one house it is "from Easter to about November." Customers who want shipment outside of this period are warned that they must take the risk of freezing. Another greenhouse says, "Shipping continues throughout the year, weather permitting." The catalogue of the third greenhouse prints this qualification: "We ship plants all months of the year except August. Plants sent for December to March 15 and during July are shipped at the customer's risk; however, we ship many orders safely during mild spells in winter."

It is clear that plants shipped during July will suffer from the heat and plants shipped during a severe cold period may freeze no matter how well they are packaged.

You may safely order in the spring and autumn. Small plants are best shipped by parcel post and it takes about a week for the journey. We would not recommend buying large plants by mail.

Damage to a plant in the preferred shipping seasons may be rectified by replacement by the greenhouse if you notify them immediately upon receipt of your plants.

It is best to ask for a catalogue before ordering. Catalogues include descriptions of plants as well as information about the minimum allowable amount of an order.

Usually directions for their immediate care are sent along with the plants. In the absence of such directions this is the procedure to follow:

Unwrap slowly and gently. Every leaf is precious when your plant is small. Water immediately with tepid water. Do not be alarmed if the bottom leaves yellow quickly. There is some trauma for plants in journeying in a closed box for several days.

Water immediately and thoroughly.

If you have a greenhouse place them there in the required light although for a few days it would be better to avoid strong, direct sunlight even though ultimately that is the required light situation. Do not fertilize them for two or three weeks until they indicate that they have recovered from their journey and are ready to take up the task of growing again. If you do not have a greenhouse, make temporary greenhouses individually or for a group as we described in Chapter IX.

Sometimes a plant which is in a two-and-one-quarter-inch or two-and-one-half-inch pot seems ready for repotting—roots are protruding from the bottom, it cannot stand upright, there seems to be no friable soil left on top. Prop it up and wait two or three weeks. Do not add the shock of repotting to the shock of travel.

The greenhouses listed below pay immediate attention to orders. They raise plants of exceptional quality and pack their material for shipment exceedingly well.

Merry Gardens	Camden, Maine 04843
M. J. Kartuz	92 Chestnut Street Wilmington, Mass. 01887
Alberts & Merkel Bros., Inc.	2210 S. Federal Highway Boynton Beach Florida 33435

For those who want ingenious watering cans and other gardening tools, a catalogue from "The House Plant Corner," Box 165–P, Oxford, Maryland, 21654, will be interesting.

For those whose enjoyment of a specific family of plants leads to the desire to learn more about that family and to specialize in it, the reference book which will list those organizations devoted to one family of plants is: *The American Directory of Horticulture* published by The American Horticultural Society, 901 N. Washington Street, Alexandria, Virginia 22314. The book is available for $5.00.

XV

What Is Your House Plant IQ?

When we read cooking recipes for the first time and try to prepare the dish it becomes a difficult task because of the need to consult the recipe again and again. Familiarity with the recipe finally makes the preparation easy and enjoyable.

Similarly, the care of your plants will become increasingly enjoyable as you become familiar with each one and with plant culture generally.

Therefore, we have prepared a quiz for you to impress certain things upon your mind and to make the answers so much your property that the sight of a certain condition in your plants will present the remedy.

1. Why do bottom leaves of a plant turn yellow and fall off?   Page 63.
2. Is there a special reason why leaves of a citrus plant become pale and then turn yellow even if they do not fall off?   Page 64.
3. Should I arrange the leaves on a plant?   Page 68.
4. Are plants benefited by having their leaves touched? Page 60.
6. How do you polish leaves?   Page 62.

29. Glazed pots protect furniture. Why do you suggest porous clay pots?   Page 31.
30. Shall I use peat pots?   Page 66.
31. What equipment do I need to repot a plant?   Page 31.
32. Which plants like to be potbound?   Page 71.
33. Why do plants grow sideways or in other directions instead of up?   Pages 61 and 66.
34. When do you rotate plants?   Page 61.
35. What do I do when soil is washed out of the pot? Page 67.
36. Books contradict each other in suggesting soils to use. What is best?   Page 51.
37. What do I do when moss appears on top of the soil and algae on pots. Are they harmful?   Page 69.
38. What can I do when surface soil becomes encrusted? Page 63.
39. How do I make feeding simple?   Page 67.
40. Do I fertilize when the light is inadequate?   Page 69.
41. Can I propagate cuttings in water?   Page 64.
42. What is air-layering? Pages 67 and 164.
43. What plants can be divided?   Page 66.
44. Can I use a milk carton for propagating or do I have to have special equipment?   Page 67.
45. If I have a plant that is not doing well when it has been correctly watered, fed, given proper light, what do I do?   Page 67.
46. What do I do to carry plants through the winter? Pages 68 and 69.
47. What is the difference between dormancy and resting? What happens in each case?   Page 36.
48. When plants are purchased from supermarkets, what should I look for to determine if it is healthy?   Page 69.
49. What should I expect from plants ordered by mail? Page 70.
50. Is there a general rule for the care of miniatures? Page 69.

51. What are worms in plants that appear when I water? Page 71.
52. What do I do when a plant falls over?   Page 69.
53. What clothes do I need for working in my greenhouse? Page 68.
54. When a plant remains wet for an abnormally long period, what do I do?   Page 58.
55. Do I water more when a plant is blooming?   Page 58.
56. How can I make my plant bloom?   Page 42.

XVI

A Sentimental Farewell

The finale of our book, like the finale of a musical work, takes us back full-cycle to our main theme—the relationship of man to nature and man's ecological responsibilities. When we garden indoors and outdoors each of us does her part in restoring ecological balance, in making our world again fit to live in. The problem has not arisen in this century. In the past as well as in the present poets and philosophers have recalled mankind to its responsibilities. Milton warned us, "Accuse not Nature! She hath done her part; do thou but thine!"[1] And Julian Huxley laid the blame where it belongs. He wrote, "Nature will no longer do the work unaided. Nature—if by that we mean blind and non-conscious forces—has, marvelously, produced man and consciousness; they must carry on the task to new results which she alone can never reach."[2]

It is time now to leave you. Shakespeare said, "One touch of nature makes the whole world kin."[3] We came together as strangers but we part in kinship, the love and knowledge of plants our common bonds. Your response to plants is greater now because response is more affirmative where there is confidence and security, two qualities we have encouraged to grow within you. "For Nature forms, and softens us within and writes our fortune's changes in our face."[4]

177

Your plants' response to you is reward for your care, fulfillment of your responsibility toward their dependence on you: you direct their growth; you chart their health and vigor; they show themselves to you in all their beauty. Oscar Wilde said it this way, "Those who find beautiful meanings in beautiful things are the cultivated. For these there is hope."[5] And Wordsworth advised us, "Come forth into the light of things. Let Nature be your teacher."[6]

We feel now like the parent who, attending the departure of one of her family, cannot refrain from last-minute counsel. Let us summarize what you have to do. We shall divide this final reminder into three parts: daily routine, weekly routine and monthly routine. Although we list one part as "daily routine," in winter it may more accurately be listed as "twice each week or even weekly." We refer to watering. As you know now, when the weather is cold and damp, it is quite possible that even for plants that like to be kept moist, you may not have to water more than twice a week—possibly even less. Their condition will depend also on the warmth of your home. However, we know that you will not rely on any watering formula. We know that you will use your eyes and your fingers to determine whether or not your plants need watering. With this repeated caution, we feel safe in listing:

DAILY ROUTINE:
>   Water plants; see if sufficient water is in pebble trays.
>   On dark days, turn on electric lights for a few hours.
>   Protect plants from freezing windowpanes by inserting
>   newspaper or plastic between plants and windows
>   at night.

WEEKLY ROUTINE:
>   Fertilize (except in the months of November and De-
>   cember).
>   Skip fertilizing if day is dark and gloomy—wait for sunny
>   day. Food does not compensate for lack of sun or light.
>   Rotate plants.
>   Stir soil with fork if it has become encrusted.

MONTHLY ROUTINE:
   Remove debris—fallen flowers, leaves.
   Wash leaves—both sides.
   Wash sides and bottom of pots.
   Pinch out if necessary.
   Prune if necessary.
   Examine plant closely to make certain it is free of pests.
   Look especially at the underside of the leaf where
      insects cluster.

Horticulture is the scence, art and cultivation of plants for ornament and use. It is our tie to the primal values of earth, air and water. It is an ancient art known to prehistoric peoples and it has been a basic occupation of mankind throughout civilization when man learned to plant and propagate plants in greater and greater variety in order to feed himself and his animals, to provide himself with medicine and fibers and finally, to endow himself with beauty.

> How often we forget all time, when lone,
> Admiring Nature's universal throne,
> Her woods, her wilds, her waters, the intense
>   reply of hers to our intelligence.[7]

In an environment that increasingly becomes urban, increasingly becomes steel and stone, increasingly artificial, we have less and less chance to know the reality of the natural world and our own place in the scheme of things. Robert Burns wrote, "Her eye intent on all the wondrous plan, she formed of various stuff the various Man."[8] Therefore, more and more, in every available space we must nurture a part of the natural world—a single plant, a small garden of plants on a windowsill, a larger garden outdoors. We have a deep psychological need for the reality of our primeval beginning—the natural world. Every contact with plants contributes to the gratification of that need.

> To him who in the love of Nature hold
> Communion with her visible forms, she speaks
> A various language.[9]

So deep is this awareness that we describe, in horticultural perceptiveness, places where we have lived happily, in contentment and tranquillity, as places where "we have sunk our roots."

Henry David Thoreau explained that he went to the woods "because I wished to front only the essential facts of life, and see if I could not learn what it had to teach and not, when I came to die, discover that I had not lived."

Walt Whitman observed his generation in America and wrote, "After you have exhausted what there is in business, politics, conviviality, and so on—and have found that none of these finally satisfy, or permanently wear—what remains? Nature remains."[10]

Much more simply, a landscape architect said recently that a garden is an experience. It is. We shall now leave you to yours.

    (1) John Milton, "Paradise Lost"
    (2) Julian Huxley, "Essays of a Biologist"
    (3) Shakespeare, "Troilus and Cressida"
    (4) Horace, "Ars Poetica"
    (5) Oscar Wilde
    (6) William Wordsworth, "The Tables Turned"
    (7) Lord Byron, "The Island"
    (8) Robert Burns, "To Robert Graham"
    (9) William Cullen Bryant, "Thanatopsis"
  (10) Walt Whitman, "Specimen Days"

Glossary of Terms

Axil—the upper angle formed by a leaf or leaf stalk and its stem.

Basal—at the base of an organ.

Bract—modified leaves intermediate between flower and the normal leaves, frequently colored.

Calyx—outer circle or cup of floral parts usually green.

Concave—hollowed out.

Coniferous—pertaining to numerous evergreens.

Cordate—heart-shaped.

Corolla—complete circle of petals.

Crenate—with teeth rounded, scalloped.

Dioecious—unisexual—the male and female reproductive organs in different plants.

Elliptical—oblong—with widest point at center.

Florets—small flowers.

Frond—leaf of fern.

Glabrous—smooth, not hairy or rough.

Glaucous—covered with white powder that rubs off.

Globose—round as a ball, globe-shaped.

Inflorescence—the flowering portion of a plant.

Lanceolate—lance-shaped, tapering toward tip.

Linear—narrow and flat with parallel margins.

Lobe—any projection of a leaf, rounded or pointed.

Node—a joint in a stalk where leaves or their vestiges are born.

Oblanceolate—broad end near tip, long tapering toward base.

Obovate—inverted ovate, the broad end upward.

Ovary—the organ which contains the ovules or rudimentary seeds which are quickened into life by the pollen. It is the hollow portion at the base of the pistil.

Palmate—veins or leaflets radiating from tip of petiole.

Panicle—an open and branched flower cluster.

Pedicel—stalk of each flower and cluster.

Peltate—leaf blade attached to stalk inside its margin.

Pendant—hanging down from its support.

Petiole—the supporting stalk of a leaf or leaf-stem.

Pinnate—feather-formed.

Pinnatifid—feathered, cut halfway to midrib.

Pistil—seed-bearing organ of the flower consisting of ovary, style and stigma.

Probiscises—elongate, protruding mouth parts of certain insects adapted for sucking or piercing.

Pubescent—covered with short, soft hairs, downy.

Raceme—elongated, simple inflorescence with stalked flowers.

Rhizomes—creeping rootstock on or under the ground.

Root—part of plant which grows down into soil and absorbs food from soil.

Scandent—climbing in whatever manner, flexuous.

Sessile—sitting close, without stalk.

Spadix—a fleshy spike bearing tiny flowers.

Spathe—a flowerlike bract partly surrounding the inflorescence

Spatulate—oblong, broadly rounded at tip but tapering to narrow base.

Stamen—the pollen-bearing or male organ.

Stellate—star-shaped; stellate hairs have radiating branches.

Stem—axis of plant which bears all other organs.

Stigma—the part of the pistil which receives the pollen grains; usually the tip of the style.

Style—is slender, tapering stalk above the ovary.

Terminal—the end or extremity of something.

Tufted—decorated with clusters of small, usually soft and flexible parts.

Umbel—inflorescence in which flower stalks or clusters arise from same point.

Undulate—wavy or wavy-margined.

General Index

Index to Plants